D1470446

AMERICA
BEFORE THE
REVOLUTION
1725–1775

Alden T. Vaughan

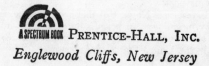

A SPECTRUM BOOK PRENTICE-HALL, INC.
Englewood Cliffs, New Jersey

TO MY FATHER
who likes to browse in early American history

Alden T. Vaughan, the editor of this volume, is Associate Professor of History at Columbia University. The author of *New England Frontier: Puritans and Indians, 1625–1675*, editor of *Chronicles of the American Revolution*, and a contributor to *Problems in American History*, Dr. Vaughans's articles and reviews have appeared in numerous historical journals and major newspapers.

E
187
.V 3

Author's Note

Americans and Europeans of the eighteenth century had not yet learned to standardize their language forms, and the resulting diversity of style gives us added insight into the colonial mind. For that reason I have wherever possible presented contemporary descriptions exactly as they were written—no matter how eccentric or inconsistent they seem to the modern eye. In a few instances, the only available version of a diary, letter, or document had already been recast into modern usage; in such cases I have reluctantly reproduced them here in their unhistorical form. Throughout, editorial comments have been inserted in square brackets. Deletion of part of a paragraph is indicated by the customary ellipses; deletion of an entire paragraph or more is shown by three centered dots.

For permission to reprint materials I am indebted to the following institutions: The New-York Historical Society and Columbia University for eighteenth-century newspaper articles and advertisements; The Historical Society of Pennsylvania for "Patrick M'Robert's Tour"; the American Historical Association for the "Journal of a French Traveler"; the University of North Carolina Press, and the Institute of Early American History and Culture, for Charles Woodmason's account of the Carolina backcountry; Fortress Press for the notebook of Henry Melchior Muhlenberg; the North Carolina State Department of Archives and History for the *Records of the Moravians in North Carolina;* the Onondaga Historical Association for *Moravian Journals Relating to Central New York;* the Henry E. Huntington Library for Robert Honyman's journal; the Massachusetts Historical Society for the journal of Josiah Quincy, Jr.; and Yale University Press for James Birket's "Cursory Remarks."

I am also indebted to several individuals who generously interrupted their own work to give me suggestions, criticisms, or clerical help. My thanks go in particular to Lawrence Cremin and his assistants at Teachers College, Columbia University, for help with the chapter on colonial education; to Joseph H. Smith of the Law School, Columbia University, for drafting the footnote that appears in the selection on colonial legal procedures; and to Michael D'Innocenzo of Hofstra University for steering me to the newspaper report on the election of Lewis Morris. Finally, this volume benefited at various stages from the attention of two talented and charming ladies—Miss Michela Eisen and Miss Barbara Bennett. To them I am especially grateful.

A. T. V.

Contents

INTRODUCTION   **1**

I. HAZARDS AND HARDSHIPS OF THE NEW WORLD   **5**

    1. The Passage to America / *Gottlieb Mittelberger*   **6**
    2. The Ravages of Epidemic Disease / *Hans and Anna Catharina Kalberlahn*   **10**
    3. The Menace of Indian Massacre / *The Moravians of North Carolina*   **12**
    4. The Discomforts of Wilderness Travel / *John C. F. Cammerhoff*   **15**
    5. The Inhumanity of Negro Slavery / *Philip Vickers Fithian*   **19**

II. LAND OF OPPORTUNITY   **23**

    6. "Excellent Good Land" / *Robert Parke*   **25**
    7. A Free Society / *Hector St. John de Crevecoeur*   **28**
    8. A Flourishing Commerce / *Robert Dinwiddie*   **31**
    9. The Benefits of Temporary Servitude / *John Harrower*   **36**
    10. The Darker Side / *Gottlieb Mittelberger and contemporary newspapers*   **42**

III. PATTERNS OF SETTLEMENT   **51**

    11. Northern Towns and Countryside / *Robert Honyman and James Birket*   **52**
    12. The Southern Patterns / *Philip Vickers Fithian and a French trader*   **56**
    13. Urban America / *Patrick M'Robert*   **63**
    14. Frontier Life / *Joseph Doddridge and Charles Woodmason*   **66**

IV. ZEAL FOR EDUCATION   73

15. Colonial School Days / *Alexander Graydon*   74
16. Self-education / *Benjamin Franklin*   79
17. The Pursuit of Useful Knowledge / *Contemporary
     newspapers*   87
18. Genesis of a Colonial College / *Samuel Johnson*   91
19. College Life / *Philip Vickers Fithian*   93

V.   THIS WORLD AND THE NEXT   97

20. A Variety of Faiths / *Peter Kalm and Ezra Stiles*   98
21. Established Religion / *William Eddis*   103
22. Remnants of Intolerance / *Charles Woodmason and
     Ezra Stiles*   105
23. Religious Indifference / *Hector St. John de Creve-
     coeur*   112
24. Religious Enthusiasm / *Nathan Cole*   114

VI. PROVINCIAL MODES OF GOVERNMENT AND LAW   117

25. Town Meeting Democracy / *Plymouth Town Rec-
     ords*   118
26. Democracy and Deference in New York / NEW
     YORK WEEKLY JOURNAL   127
27. An Element of Monarchy / BOSTON WEEKLY NEWS-
     LETTER   131
28. Political Friction: Colony v. Crown / *George Clin-
     ton*   133
29. Political Friction: Seaboard v. Backcountry / *Henry
     Melchior Muhlenberg*   135
30. The Administration of Justice, American Style /
     Joseph Bennett   141

VII. ARTS AND ENTERTAINMENT   147

31. Emergence of an American Theater / PENNSYL-
     VANIA CHRONICLE AND UNIVERSAL ADVERTISER   149

32. Culture and Diversion in the Cities / *Josiah Quincy, Jr. and Joseph Bennett*   150

33. Social Life on a Virginia Plantation / *Philip Vickers Fithian*   156

34. Frontier Pastimes / *Joseph Doddridge*   158

35. The King of Sports / *J. F. D. Smyth*   163

36. A Growing Taste for Literature / *Contemporary newspapers*   165

VIII.   PERSPECTIVES AND PREDICTIONS   171

37. Happiness, Not Empire / *Andrew Burnaby*   172

38. "Past, Present, and Future" / *Nathaniel Ames*   175

39. Prospects of Political and Economic Independence / *William Eddis*   178

40. A New Society / *Hector St. John de Crevecoeur*   182

Introduction

The United States of America is not unique in having undergone a long colonial status. Almost half of today's nations were at one time colonies of another country—and the present character of those nations depends in large part on the kind of growth they experienced while under foreign domination. Fortunately for the United States, its colonial period was marked more by expansion than by exploitation, more by maturation than by servile dependency. As a result, the venture of 1776 in which thirteen colonies declared themselves "free and independent states" owed its success as much to the provincial heritage as to the ability of its leaders. In Colonial America lay the roots of the American Republic.

For more than 150 years America evolved under British rule. The first half of that period was primarily a time of settlement: hardy settlers carved new colonies out of the American forest which rapidly filled with immigrants from the British Isles and Europe. The sparse native population was pushed aside or overridden, so that its impact on the new societies remained slight. Wherever colonies took root, they were at first mere offshoots of Europe—for the most part distant extensions of seventeenth-century England. And as the colonies grew at various speeds and in various ways the stamp of the mother country remained clear. Yet slowly—almost imperceptibly to those who witnessed the events—a transformation was taking place.

By mid-eighteenth century British America had become conspicuously American. No longer were the thirteen mainland colonies mere microcosms of the mother country; no longer was an American simply a transplanted Englishman. So extensively had the colonists modified the customs and institutions they brought with them, and so far had the ethnic composition of the settlers evolved since the seventeenth century, that America, though still loyal and subservient

1

to the British Crown, could claim to be a distinct society: a curious blend of European peoples and customs and institutions, mixed in varying arrangements, and modified in many subtle but significant respects by the influence of the New World itself.

The uniqueness of America showed itself in countless ways. Most obvious was its ethnic distribution, now no longer exclusively British; enclaves of German, French, Scandinavian, Dutch, and Spanish settlers—to mention but a few nationalities—were interspersed among the emigrants from the British Isles. And no longer was the British element so predominantly English. Welshmen, Irishmen, Scots (from both Scotland and northern Ireland) toiled alongside Americans who traced their ancestral roots to London or East Anglia.

Still more variety could be found in religious affiliations: Baptists, Lutherans, Presbyterians, Catholics, and Jews (not to mention some of the more esoteric sects) endured, if they did not flourish, alongside the Quakers of Pennsylvania, the Congregationalists of New England, and the Anglicans of Virginia. Europe, to be sure, had given birth to each of America's religious groups, but to no part of the world did they come in such plenitude as to America, where people were learning toleration as a necessity of life and where they could practice religious exclusiveness only until another sect took up land nearby.

At the same time, America was becoming conspicuous for its material opportunities, marked by a general prosperity with few pockets of either poverty or opulence. Every American colony had its rich and its poor, but the extremes were less marked than in Europe, and the criteria for achieving a station in life emphasized individual accomplishment more than circumstances of birth. Similarly, America's social structure had few rigidities and few extremes. A land which knew no titled nobility and in which the oldest family had been newcomers only a few generations earlier had little on which to base social distinctions except wealth—usually self-earned—and personal or professional qualities.

By the second quarter of the eighteenth century, British America had also evolved its own peculiar political forms. Of great significance was the American's frequent opportunity to choose his public officials, usually through annual elections, for all colonies enjoyed a remarkably broad franchise. Equally significant was the application of the British parliamentary formula to the administration of the colonies: in each a miniature House of Commons controlled the public purse and struggled for power (usually successfully) with the upper house and the representative of the Crown. Americans also were developing their own approaches to local government and to the administration of civil and criminal law.

Least distinctive in America's emergence as a separate society was her culture, at least in the narrow sense of that term. Obviously a society building its foundations is too busy to spend much time perfecting friezes, chandeliers, and cornice pieces. High culture, and the training to appreciate and produce it, had to come mostly from the Old World. But if American culture continued to be largely derivative, it at least began to be uniquely American in selection. Usefulness supplanted beauty as the major criterion as an American aesthetic pragmatism emerged in the eighteenth century. This could readily be seen in American education, in American craftsmanship, in American architecture, and in the mainstream of an emerging American literature.

This volume provides a glimpse of America at the height of its colonial experience. It lets the colonists and their contemporaries describe the aspects of America which they knew firsthand; from their accounts emerges a composite picture of Colonial America in the half-century before the Revolution. The editor has purposely avoided selections that emphasize the approaching clash between Great Britain and her American colonies; instead, the focus of this volume is on the thirteen mainland provinces during the fifty-year period in which they exhibited an appreciable degree of maturity and stability—at least in comparison with the erratic century that came before. While eschewing direct comment on the impending revolution, this collection of readings nevertheless reveals a vitality and prosperity in the American colonies which encouraged thoughts of independence, and a society so deeply appreciated by its inhabitants that in 1775 they would fight for its preservation.

I

Hazards and Hardships
of the New World

Colonial Americans were, of necessity, a hardy lot. The American wilderness, still largely untamed in the eighteenth century, offered great trials as well as great opportunities, and the settlers again and again found themselves pitted against forces of man and nature. For some the struggle was too hard, and they succumbed to untimely death or returned to the Old World. But most survived with tenacity their struggle against an environment which offered—especially on the frontier—as much threat as promise.

For many Colonial Americans the first and most dangerous challenge lay in the three thousand miles of ocean that separated the old home from the new. For others the experience of the passage came secondhand but was poignant nonetheless, for they heard of it from parents or friends for whom the voyage had been a harrowing event. Of course, by mid-eighteenth century there were thousands of families that could boast—if that was their wont—of lineage back to the early seventeenth century. But for every such "old timer" there was a score of the newly-arrived. Indelibly impressed in their memories were the agonies of a sea voyage that lasted as long as two months, was fraught with danger and discomfort, and for countless hundreds had been the end of their experience with the New World rather than the beginning of a new life.

For survivors of the passage, arrival in America did not mean an end to all torments. Perhaps life for the immigrant became more pleasant and more hopeful than it had been in the Old World, but it was more dangerous as well. The New World contained abundant hazards and hardships that plagued the life of all Americans—those

5

who could trace their American ancestry back several generations no less than those who had just arrived. There were, for example, the aborigines who were often hostile (often justly so) and who waged a particularly terrifying kind of warfare. Too, the colonies harbored a host of fatal diseases not common to Europe. And for the tens of thousands of colonists of African Negro blood (whose voyage to America was involuntary as well as abnormally perilous) the New World offered the additional hardship of human slavery—with its appalling physical and psychological hazards. Thus in most colonists —new and old, black and white—there developed a heightened awareness of human frailty and vulnerability. In the decades before the Revolution that awareness became a distinctive characteristic of the colonial mind.

1.—THE PASSAGE TO AMERICA

Encouraged by stories of phenomenal abundance and opportunity—sometimes true, but often exaggerated by agents who were paid to sign up passengers—men, women, and children from every nation flocked to European seaports to take passage to America. But as this excerpt from Gottlieb Mittelberger's Journey to Pennsylvania in the Year 1750 reveals, the trip to the New World could be painful, disillusioning, and often fatal.—From Gottlieb Mittelberger's Journey to Pennsylvania in the Year 1750 . . . , *tr. Carl T. Eben. (Philadelphia, 1898), pp. 18-24.*

[The entire journey from Germany to Pennsylvania, via Holland and England,] lasts from the beginning of May to the end of October, fully half a year, amid such hardships as no one is able to describe adequately with their misery.

The cause is because the Rhine-boats from Heilbronn to Holland have to pass by 36 custom-houses, at all of which the ships are examined, which is done when it suits the convenience of the custom-house officials. In the meantime the ships with the people are detained long, so that the passengers have to spend much money. The trip down the Rhine alone lasts therefore 4, 5 and even 6 weeks.

When the ships with the people come to Holland, they are detained there likewise 5 or 6 weeks. Because things are very dear there, the poor people have to spend nearly all they have during that time. Not to mention many sad accidents which occur here; having seen with my own eyes how a man, as he was about to board the ship near Rotterdam, lost two children at once by drowning.

Both in Rotterdam and in Amsterdam the people are packed densely, like herrings so to say, in the large sea-vessels. One person receives a place of scarcely 2 feet width and 6 feet length in the bedstead, while many a ship carries four to six hundred souls; not to mention the innumerable implements, tools, provisions, water-barrels and other things which likewise occupy much space.

On account of contrary winds it takes the ships sometimes 2, 3 and 4 weeks to make the trip from Holland to Cowes in England. But when the wind is good, they get there in 8 days or even sooner. Everything is examined there and the custom-duties paid, whence it comes that the ships ride there 8, 10 to 14 days and even longer at anchor, till they have taken in their full cargoes. During that time every one is compelled to spend his last remaining money and to consume his little stock of provisions which had been reserved for the sea; so that most passengers, finding themselves on the ocean where they would be in greater need of them, must greatly suffer from hunger and want. Many suffer want already on the water between Holland and Old England.

When the ships have for the last time weighed their anchors near the city of Cowes in England, the real misery begins with the long voyage. For from there the ships, unless they have good wind, must often sail 8, 9, 10 to 12 weeks before they reach Philadelphia. But even with the best wind the voyage lasts 7 weeks.

But during the voyage there is on board these ships terrible misery, stench, fumes, horror, vomiting, many kinds of sea-sickness, fever, dysentery, headache, heat, constipation, boils, scurvy, cancer, mouth-rot, and the like, all of which come from old and sharply salted food and meat, also from very bad and foul water, so that many die miserably.

Add to this want of provisions, hunger, thirst, frost, heat, dampness, anxiety, want, afflictions and lamentations, together with other trouble, as for example the lice abound so frightfully, especially on sick people, that they can be scraped off the body. The misery reaches the climax when a gale rages for 2 or 3 nights and days, so that every one believes that the ship will go to the bottom with all human beings on board. In such a visitation the people cry and pray most piteously.

When in such a gale the sea rages and surges, so that the waves rise often like high mountains one above the other, and often tumble over the ship, so that one fears to go down with the ship; when the ship is constantly tossed from side to side by the storm and waves, so that no one can either walk, or sit, or lie, and the closely packed people in the berths are thereby tumbled over each other, both the sick and the well—it will be readily understood that many of these people, none of whom had been prepared for hardships, suffer so terribly from them that they do not survive it.

I myself had to pass through a severe illness at sea, and I best know how I felt at the time. These poor people often long for consolation, and I often entertained and comforted them with singing, praying and exhorting; and whenever it was possible and the winds and waves permitted it, I kept daily prayer-meetings with them on deck. Besides, I baptized five children in distress, because we had no ordained minister on board. I also held divine service every Sunday by reading sermons to the people; and when the dead were sunk in the water, I commended them and our souls to the mercy of God.

Among the healthy, impatience sometimes grows so great and cruel that one curses the other, or himself and the day of his birth, and sometimes come near killing each other. Misery and malice join each other, so that they cheat and rob one another. One always reproaches the other with having persuaded him to undertake the journey. Frequently children cry out against their parents, husbands against their wives and wives against their husbands, brothers and sisters, friends and acquaintances against each other. But most against the soul-traffickers.

Many sigh and cry: "Oh, that I were at home again, [even] if I had to lie in my pig-sty!" Or they say: "O God, if I only had a piece of good bread, or a good fresh drop of water." Many people whimper, sigh and cry piteously for their homes; most of them get home-sick. Many hundred people necessarily die and perish in such misery, and must be cast into the sea, which drives their relatives, or those who persuaded them to undertake the journey, to such despair that it is almost impossible to pacify and console them. In a word, the sighing and crying and lamenting on board the ship continues night and day, so as to cause the hearts even of the most hardened to bleed when they hear it.

No one can have an idea of the sufferings which women in confinement have to bear with their innocent children on board these ships. Few of this class escape with their lives; many a mother is cast into the water with her child as soon as she is dead. One day, just as we had a heavy gale, a woman in our ship, who was to give birth and could not give birth under the circumstances, was pushed through a [port-hole] in the ship and dropped into the sea, because she was far in the rear of the ship and could not be brought forward. Children from 1 to 7 years rarely survive the voyage; and many a time parents are compelled to see their children miserably suffer and die from hunger, thirst and sickness, and then to see them cast into the water. I witnessed such misery in no less than 32 children in our ship, all of whom were thrown into the sea. The parents grieve all the more since their children find no resting-place in the earth, but are devoured by the monsters of the sea. It is a notable fact that children, who have not yet had the measles or small-pocks, generally get them on board the ship, and mostly die of them.

Often a father is separated by death from his wife and children, or mothers from their little children, or even both parents from their children; and sometimes whole families die in quick succession; so that often many dead persons lie in the berths beside the living ones, especially when contagious diseases have broken out on board the ship.

Many other accidents happen on board these ships, especially by falling, whereby people are often made cripples and can never be set right again. Some have also fallen into the ocean.

That most of the people get sick is not surprising, because, in addition to all other trials and hardships, warm food is served only three times a week, the rations being very poor and very little. Such meals can hardly be eaten, on account of being so unclean. The water which is served out of the ships is often very black, thick and full of worms, so that one cannot drink it without loathing, even with the greatest thirst. O surely, one would often give much money at sea for a piece of good bread, or a drink of good water, not to say a drink of good wine, if it were only to be had. I myself experienced that sufficiently, I am sorry to say. Toward the end we were compelled to eat the ship's biscuit which had been spoiled long ago; though in a whole biscuit there was scarcely a piece the size of a dollar that had not been full of red worms and spiders' nests. Great hunger and thirst force us to eat and drink everything; but many a one does so at the risk of his life. The sea-water cannot be drunk, because it is salt and bitter as gall. If this were not so, such a voyage could be made with less expense and without so many hardships.

At length, when, after a long and tedious voyage, the ships come in sight of land, so that the promonotories can be seen, which the people were so eager and anxious to see, all creep from below on deck to see the land from afar, and they weep for joy, and pray and sing, thanking and praising God.

2.—THE RAVAGES
OF EPIDEMIC DISEASE

In the eighteenth century medical science in Europe as well as in America could do little to prevent periodic epidemics. Yet in Europe, aside from a few notable exceptions, epidemics were confined to the large cities; the relative cleanliness and isolation of rural areas kept most Europeans from exposure until they sailed for the New World. Some, as seen in Mittelberger's account, encountered fatal diseases en route. Many others survived the voyage only to succumb in America, where new conditions, new diet, and new causative agents frequently triggered minor maladies into frightening epidemics. The following account of an epidemic in North Carolina in 1759 was compiled from the memoirs of a doctor, Hans Kalberlahn, and the autobiography of his wife, Anna Catharina.—From Adelaide L. Fries, ed., Records of the Moravians in North Carolina, I (1752-1771) (Raleigh, 1922), pp. 221-222.

In time peace [with the Indians] was restored . . . but before that day a great wave of affliction had passed over Bethabara [North Carolina]. Typhus fever became epidemic in parts of North Carolina and Virginia, persisting for five or six months, and Bethabara, crowded with refugees, constantly exposed to infection from the strangers who came and went, suffered severely. Nothing that the doctors could do checked the disease, scarcely alleviated the suffering, as one after another sickened, and only nineteen of the inhabitants escaped a more or less serious attack.

Mary Rogers, wife of the English-speaking minister of the Parish, was the first to die. She had been in feeble health ever since the birth of her little daughter Salome, and fell an easy victim to the fever, passing away after a brief illness, and leaving her six-months-old baby to Sister Kalberlahn, who promised to care for it as though it were her own. Then Christian Seidel's bride was borne up the steep path, and laid to rest upon the hilltop, facing the east. Her husband, broken-hearted but brave, went on with his work, but within a week returned from a visit to the new village with the fever on him, and laid himself down to die. It did not seem a serious case and hope was entertained for his recovery, but he calmly said "It is the end, life was lonely without my Catherine, and on the way to Bethania I prayed my God to take me to himself."

And Dr. Kalberlahn, worn from his long journey, spent with watching, grieving for his friends, was tortured with an agony of helplessness such as he had never known before. Scorching tears burst from his eyes as he fell on his knees before the Lord, praying, praying, praying for knowledge how to aid these dearly beloved Brethren who never yet had looked to him in vain.

Then he too was stricken, and with the summons there came a strange, sweet peace. The burden of responsibility was lifted; calmly he arranged his earthly affairs; with childlike faith he committed himself and all he loved to his Saviour's care; then for two almost happy days he lay with his wife's hand in his, cheering her with loving, tender words. . . .

And Sister Kalberlahn was not alone in her half-stunned sorrow. There were many anxious, aching, hearts in Bethabara, asking why the Lord should have sent this plague upon them, why have taken from them their pastor, their doctor, and all these others, whose graves were being made in the consecrated plots here and by the mill. Gottlieb Reuter, a boyhood friend of Seidel, found comfort in the thought expressed in a few stanzas, faulty in metre, somewhat crude in phrase, but with true poesy in the picture of the "hundred-thousand acre field" now sanctified by tears, where the reapers were passing to and fro, seeking souls ripe for a heavenly garner, and bearing them up to present before the Throne as the first-fruits of Wachovia.

> I dreamed:—Two angels by me stood,
>   As on a bed of pain I lay,
> "*He* is not ripe," one softly said.
>   But that night CHRISTIAN passed away.
> Two Sisters had already gone
>   Unto eternal mansions blest;
> And two days later KALBERLAHN
>   Entered into his heavenly rest.
> Bethabara was sore distressed.
>   Again I dreamed:—I heard a voice;
> "My little flock, be not dismayed,

But, even in your woe, rejoice.
This hundred-thousand-acre field
Now truly consecrate shall be;
Therefore the angel-reapers come
To bear the first-fruits home for me."
Lord Jesus Christ, Thou art so true,
Thou art so merciful to all,
We pray for grace Thy will to do,
To trust Thy love whate'er befall.

3.—THE MENACE
OF INDIAN MASSACRE

The hazards of the New World were not confined to such incomprehensible agents as disease or weather. Often they took human form, for the threat of Indian attack became a frightening adjunct to the westward movement. Red man and white were not always locked in mortal combat, but increasingly in the eighteenth century war whoops and musket fire echoed along the provincial frontier. The following account is from the records for 1760 of two Moravian church settlements, Wachovia and Bethabara, in North Carolina.—From Adelaide L. Fries, ed., Records of the Moravians in North Carolina, *I (1752-1771) (Raleigh, 1922), pp. 227-230.*

[Wachovia]

This was a year of fierce Indian war, and on the 10th of February the first whites were killed by the Cherokees in North Carolina; on the 26th of February they attacked Fort Dobbs; and March 8th they killed William Fish and his son a few miles from here. Under these circumstances, we doubled the Watch. The Texts of Feb. 28th and March 9th became true of us before we came to them in our reading: "Neither Nehemiah nor his brethren put off their clothes, (Neh. IV: 23) but prayed as they watched." "They appointed watches of the inhabitants," (Neh. VII:3). On the 12th of March many Indians were in our neighborhood; eight miles away, on the Yadkin, houses were burned; two men were killed at the bridge over the Wach; two persons were killed on the Town Fork. They had one large camp six miles from Bethania, and a smaller one less than three miles. Here, at the mill, and at Bethania, there were Indians spies every night. March 16th, a beautiful snow fell, lying for several days, and then we could see the smoke from their camps. Among our neighbors more than fifteen people were slain. The Indians said later that they had tried to make prisoners here, but had failed; that several times they had been stopped by the sound of the watchman's horn and the ringing of the bell for morning and evening services. In their own country they starved out Fort Louden and took the entire garrison captive.

❦

[Bethabara]

January and the first two weeks of February were quiet so far as Indians were concerned, the news being that the Cherokees had made peace with South Carolina and had given hostages for good behaviour. . . .

•   •   •

On the same day [Feb. 14] Indian alarms began again, and as they seemed well founded, Bethania was at once notified. On the 19th refugees came telling of great alarm on the Yadkin, and two days later letters from Major Dunn and others to Jacob Loesch reported the country about Salisbury much disturbed, and that a large party of Indians was believed to be making its way along the hills to the Yadkin. The stockade at the mill was repaired, a watch set there and in Bethabara, and preparations made for the defense of Bethania, should the foe attack there. Powder was sent from Fort Dobbs for the Bethabara Fort. Actual traces of Indians were seen for the first time, on the 25th, some miles from Bethabara.

March was a very trying month. On the 4th news came that in the preceding week the Indians had tried to lure the soldiers outside Fort Dobbs and there had been a fight. . . . On the 9th a man came, pierced through and through with an arrow. He related that 24 hours before William Fish and his son had asked him to go with them to their farm to get provisions for the families gathered at a certain place on the Yadkin. Some miles up the river they happened upon a party of Indians, who fired at them and then shot many arrows. Fish and his son fell, but this man, longing to reach Bethabara, for his soul's sake rode into the river to escape them. On the further side he found more Indians, but they paid no attention to him and he recrossed the river, plunged into the woods, where in the darkness and rain he soon lost his way, and wounded by two arrows wandered for many hours, but finally reached the Moravian town where Dr. Bonn took out the arrow and saved his life. The next day 50 persons, who had gathered on the Yadkin, came to the Bethabara Fort for protection. On the 11th a company of militia passed through, going to the Yadkin to bury William Fish and his son. However, they found the Indians out in force, so let the burial go and contented themselves with visiting the families who had thought to hold their ground, and bringing them to the fort. Next day a messenger came from the Town Fork, where another group of settlers was surrounded, and the militia went to bring them in also, but returned on the 13th with the news that two men had been killed and the rest had escaped. The next night Indians were seen in Bethania; the watchman shot at them and drove them off, then there arose a strong wind and on it came the sound as of the howling of a hundred wolves. On the night of the 15th a snow fell, which stopped the activities of the Indians for a few days; otherwise the danger continued. One of the refugees narrowly escaped death on the path between Bethabara and Bethania; two others going out against the advice of Brother Anspach, who was in command at the mill, were attacked and one of them killed. Larger parties of the refugees went out at times to secure food and see how matters were going. Frequently spies were seen about the fort and mill. On the 20th, word came that John Thomas, a Baptist minister, had been killed between the Wach and the Ens, on the road to Ebits Creek; another of the party was missing, while the third escaped.

April 2nd letters from Fort Dobbs acknowledged the receipt of letters from Bethabara and stated that Mr. Long had been killed on his way back from the Fort. On the same day announcement was made of various candidates for the office of Burgess from this County. Col. Hunt and ten men came about this and told us a good deal about the condition of things outside of Wachovia. It has seemed as though we were the only ones left in this neighborhood, and Col. Hunt said that at least half the inhabitants had fled from the County.

4.—THE DISCOMFORTS
OF WILDERNESS TRAVEL

Among the hardships that characterized Colonial America was difficulty of travel. Newcomers complained of it, old settlers took weary note of it, and all agreed that almost everywhere—along the Post Road from Boston to New York as well as through the rugged inland trails—travel was slow, uncomfortable, and often dangerous. The journey through the back country of New York in 1750, described in the "Diary of the Journey of Brother Cammerhoff and David Zeisberger . . . ," reveals the difficulties travelers frequently encountered.—From W. M. Beauchamp, ed., Moravian Journals Relating to Central New York, 1745-66 *(Syracuse, 1916), pp. 36-39, 65-68.*

[*Saturday, 2-13* June* [*1750*]]. . . . We started off again, but were obliged to cross the creek twice. We tried to ford it on our horses, but might have had a dreadful accident, for they were wild and untrained, and had scarcely been used, so that we were in great danger. The road we had to take was a very strange one, such as I had never yet seen anywhere in this country, and difficult to describe to anyone unacquainted in this wilderness. The underbrush was so dense that we could scarcely see daylight; many thousand immense trees lay on the road, which the horses had either to go around or jump over. We were obliged to cross the creek about thirty times, and generally waded through it. Beside all this there were many marshy, muddy places. Notwithstanding these difficulties we felt encouraged to go on, being sure of the Lord's presence. After we had continued for some time in the valley, we ascended a wild and rocky clift, and when we had reached the mountain, which was very high, the Gajuka [Indian guide] prepared our dinner. Though at a great

---

* The diarist recorded dates in both Old Style (Julian Calendar) and New Style (Gregorian Calendar), which in the eighteenth century differed by eleven days.

height yet we had no view at all, because of the dense forest around us, so wild and dark that we might have supposed ourselves in a deep valley. We refreshed ourselves with some Indian corn, which we had boiled in the morning, and which the Gajuka had carried here on his back. We had no water, as there was none to be found here. We thought specially of our friends in Bethlehem and Gnadenhutten to-day. We named our quarters the Indian Sabbath Lodgings, and again started off on our way. As the road was very bad and dangerous here, the Gajuka led us for some time through the forest, over the fallen trees and through the bushes, so that sometimes we could scarcely find our way out. We crept along as well as we could, and after having gone on a few miles more we came to the road, and again found water. It was, however, all a wilderness, and we passed through swamps, marshes and bushes. As the weather was very cloudy it increased the darkness, so that at times we might have supposed that night was coming on. We passed through a neighborhood which the Indians called Kassickahe, because of the tall trees there. It is true that there are a great many there, and of such a height as can hardly be imagined. There were three posts painted red, on which the Indians had fastened by their feet, according to their usual custom, the three Gatabes [enemy Indians] whom they had taken prisoners.

We built ourselves a good, secure hut, and the Gajuka did the same, for we expected rain. We named our quarters the Tabernacle in the War Camp. David and I remembered how wonderfully we had been led over strange and difficult paths, and then retired to rest. It rained very hard all night.

Sunday, 3-14 June. . . . It was very wet in the morning. It never gets very dry in this wilderness, as the sun cannot penetrate the thick forest. We started, notwithstanding the dampness. Our way led us, like yesterday, over the mountains, through swamps and valleys, and finally to a lake, which was not very large, but yet several miles in circumference. Toward the south it empties into the Owego [Oswego?] creek. The Indians have named it Ganiatarenge. Here we rested, and the Gajuka gave us some geographical information, telling us that from here, W. and W. N. W., we were not far from the land of the Sennekas. He said it was four days' journey from Gajuka N. W. to the French, five days' journey to a large river named Gatarochqui, wider than the Delaware at Philadelphia. This river flowed from Lake Niagara, famous for its large falls. He described the falls as being as high as if we were to place four or five pine trees one upon the other, (we saw some here which were certainly more than 100 feet high), and said that he had been there four times.

• • •

This is the first warm day we have had since leaving Wajomik, and we perspired freely, going down the mountain into the country called by the Indians Tianontinaou. We were overtaken by a very heavy shower and thunder-storm, but went on notwithstanding, and came to a beautiful spring, to which we gave the name of Pentecostal Spring. We took our dinner there. Then we traveled on, and were again overtaken by a heavy shower and thunder-storm. As night was coming on we built ourselves a hut near a creek named Sto-ke, at a place where much sugar has been boiled. We succeeded in getting our things under roof before the rain. We spent a happy evening together.

Monday, 4-15 June. It rained during the whole night, and continued as hard this morning, with a heavy wind-storm, so that it seemed at times as if we would be obliged to remain here, and we had no desire to do this. A few Indian women from Ganatocheracht came to us; they had left there shortly after we did. We then resolved to start on our way, although the shower had not ceased, and everything was very wet. Our road was very bad; it lay through swamps and marshes, and was made almost impassable at times by the fallen trees, so that at times we scarcely knew how to proceed. At last we reached the foot of a high mountain, called by the Indians Untagechiat, and came out of the forest, (where we had traveled for three days, and in which we had not had any view at all) into an open plain. . . .

• • •

. . . [*Saturday, 27 June*]. . . . We . . . took leave of our hosts in Indian fashion, and went with our Gajuka to the lake, which was pretty rough and broke in great waves, it being quite windy. We got into our bark canoe and set off. Some Indians in another canoe went with us to Nuquiage. Our bark vessel danced around bravely on the waves, and the water came in freely, as the lake was very wild. Near the shore the water was green, but in the middle it was blue as the ocean, and the Indians say it may be 20 to 30 fathoms deep. . . .

We crossed the lake in about two hours, landed, and then started on our way. It was again intensely hot. Our course lay west by north and west northwest. We soon entered a wilderness, which we called the Dry Desert, because we found no water, and were obliged to suffer from great thirst on account of the intense heat. At last, after we had walked about 20 miles, we came to the first running water,

which Gallichwio [Cammerhoff's Indian name] named the Golden
Brook, because, although the water was rather warm, it tasted so
good to him. We continued our journey and walked very fast, from
14 to 15 miles, again without water. At last we came to a creek called
Ganazioha, where we found an Indian, who had procured rum from
a French trader living farther on, near Lake Nuquiage. We went on
and arrived about an hour before sunset at Nuquiage, a Gajuka town.
The Indians went directly toward the house of the French trader,
who fills the whole neighborhood with his rum. Then we went into
it also, and he bade us welcome. He immediately offered us roasted
eels, and made us punch to drink. . . .

•   •   •

Sunday, 17-28 June. Early in the morning it was very wet and
warm. We made an early start. Our course lay west southwest; we
came into the land of the Sennekas, which borders on that of the
Gajukas. . . .

. . . We had a worse road than we had on the whole journey.
The Gajuka told us, in starting, that we would have to pass over a
bad road, and if he said the road was bad, it must certainly be *very*
bad. Thus far we had at least been able to travel on the ground, but
now we went through swamps and marshes, where the flies troubled
us greatly. For miles we were obliged to walk on trees and branches,
as on both sides were deep marshes, bushes and thorns, which make
an inconvenient bridge, for we sometimes slipped from the trees and
branches, and fell into the swamp, and could scarcely get up again
with our heavy bundles. We called the road the Long Bridge. It
would have been quite impassable with horses, and the Indians say
no one can travel this road except on foot. After we had continued in
this swamp for about six miles we came to a creek, called Axoquenta
or Firestone Creek. From thence the road was a little better. Toward
evening we reached an old Indian settlement, where a city by the
name of Onnachee is said to have stood, but which is now uninhabited.
We were caught in a dreadful thunder and rain storm, and were
thoroughly drenched, particularly in going through the tall grass.
We went on a little farther and encamped along a creek called
Otochshiaco. David built a hut as best he could, with the little bark
to be found. We tried to dry ourselves at the fire, and called our
quarters Senneka Mail Station, and went to sleep, feeling cold and
wet.

5.—THE INHUMANITY
OF NEGRO SLAVERY

*The hardships of travel, disease, and Indian attack were a
threat to all Colonial Americans. But for some twenty per
cent of the population the cruelties of slavery added a peculiar hardship. (The hardships of bondage were experienced by white indentured servants too, but rarely to the
same extent, and their terms were seldom for more than a
few years; by 1750 their numbers had declined while those
of Negro slaves had sharply accelerated.) Philip Vickers
Fithian, a Yale graduate serving as tutor to the family of
Robert Carter in Virginia, recorded a Northerner's impression of human bondage in America.—From John
Rogers Williams, ed.,* Philip Vickers Fithian: Journal and
Letters, 1767-1774 *(Princeton, 1900), pp. 68-69, 135-136,
151, 255.*

[*Thursday, 23 December 1773*]. . . . This Evening, after I had
dismissed the Children, & was sitting in the School-Room cracking
Nuts, none present but Mr. *Carters Clerk,* a civil, inoffensive, agreeable young Man, who acts both in the character of a Clerk and
Steward, when the Woman who makes my Bed, asked me for the
key of my Room, and on seeing the young Man sitting with me, she
told him that her Mistress had this afternoon given orders that their
Allowance of Meat should be given out to them to-morrow.—She
left us; I then asked the young man what their allowance is? He told
me that, excepting some favourites about the table their weekly allowance is a peck of Corn, & a pound of Meat a Head!—And Mr.
Carter is allowed by all, & from what I have already seen of others,
I make no Doubt at all but he is, by far the most humane to his
Slaves of any in these parts! Good God! are these Christians?—
When I am on the Subject, I will relate further, what I heard Mr.
George Lees Overseer, one Morgan, say the other day that he himself
had often done to Negroes, and found it useful; He said that whipping
of any kind does them no good, for they will laugh at your greatest

Severity; But he told us he had invented two things, and by several experiments had proved their success.—For Sulleness, Obstinacy, or Idleness, says he, Take a Negro, strip him, tie him fast to a post; take then a sharp Curry-Comb, & curry him severely til he is well scraped; & call a Boy with some dry Hay, and make the Boy rub him down for several Minutes, then salt him, & unlose him. He will attend to his Business, (said the inhuman Infidel) afterwards!—But savage Cruelty does not exceed His next diabolical invention—To get a Secret from a Negro, says he, take the following Method— Lay upon your Floor a large thick plank, having a peg about eighteen Inches long, of hard wood, & very Sharp, on the upper end, fixed fast in the plank—then strip the Negro, tie the Cord to a staple in the Ceiling, so as that his foot may just rest on the sharpened Peg, then turn him briskly round, and you would laugh (said our informer) at the Dexterity of the Negro, while he was relieving his Feet on the sharpened Peg!—I need say nothing of these seeing there is a righteous God, who will take vengeance on such Inventions! . . .

· · ·

Thursday, 24 [March 1774]. At Breakfast Mr. Carter entertained us with an account of what he himself saw the other Day, which is a strong Representation of the cruelty & distress which many among the Negroes suffer in Virginia!

Mr. Carter dined at Squire Lees some few Weeks ago; at the same place, that day, dined also Mr. George Turburville & his Wife —As Mr. Carter rode up he observed Mr. Turburville's Coach-Man sitting on the Chariot-Box, the Horses off—After he had made his compliments in the House, he had occasion soon after to go to the Door, when he saw the Coachman still sitting, & on examination found that he was there fast chained! The Fellow is inclined to run away, & this is the method which This Tyrant makes use of to keep him when abroad; & So soon as he goes home he is delivered into the pityless Hands of a bloody Overseer! . . .

· · ·

[Sunday, 10 April 1774]. . . . Before Breakfast I saw a Ring of Negroes at the Stable, fighting Cocks, and in several parts of the plantation they are digging up their small Lots of ground allow'd by their Master for Potatoes, peas, &c; All such work for themselves they constantly do on Sundays, as they are otherwise employed on every other Day. . . .

· · ·

[Saturday, 17 September 1774]. . . . Ben [Carter, Robert Carter's

son] returned about seven from Westmoreland Courthouse—He informed us that Mr. *Sorrels* Negroes had their trial there to Day, concerning their accusation of entering their Masters House in the night with an intention to murder Him—It was there proved (so far as Negroes evidence will go) that a Brother of this Sorrel early last Spring bribed some Negroes to Poison his Brother; & when that diabolical Attempt could not succeed, he has since tried to perswade them to murder Him!—But all evidence against the Negroes was so weak & dark that the judges ordered them to be whiped & dismissed them—Though the Law considers all Testimony given by a Negro against a White-Man as weak & unsubstantial; yet what the Negro said to Day on Oath of the younger Mr. Sorrel, seems to gain much Belief with many who are candid & unbiased Judges. . . .

II

Land
of Opportunity

If eighteenth-century America offered hazards and hardships, it also offered unparalleled opportunity. Especially to the oppressed of Europe, the British mainland colonies promised a chance to start life anew under more auspicious surroundings than they had known before. In America a man might find the success and fortune that in the Old World proved elusive to all but a chosen few.

For most Colonial Americans the immediate goal was economic prosperity. Surrounded by an abundance of land, a shortage of labor, and a flexible system of apprenticeship, a man could expect to live more comfortably than had his father; his own son would almost certainly surpass both. That was the hope that lured tens of thousands of Europeans to America's shore. And in the half-century from 1725 to 1775, the possibility was tantamount to probability.

Land was the keystone in the arch of opportunity. There was so much—as much as in all of Europe. And it was so cheap—at least the uncleared tracts along the frontier. Moreover, the readiness with which a man could cease laboring for others and go to work on land of his own caused wages in almost every occupation to become double or treble what they had been at home. Of course, possession of farmland did not assure prosperity; it required a lifetime of labor, and the farmer's toil was forever at the mercy of drought, a fickle market, or (on the outer fringes of settlement) Indian attack. Still, a family that owned even the meanest land could be reasonably sure of adequate food, shelter, and clothing. That was more than most settlers had had in the Old World.

Of course, not every American took to the soil. For many the sea beckoned more temptingly, with its own promise of material reward and high adventure. Hundreds of fishing towns and commercial ports dotted Colonial America's two-thousand-mile coastline, where seafaring colonists found profit and excitement. And for landlubbers who liked the smell of the sea, the port towns offered employment for ropemakers, sailmakers, shipwrights, warehousemen, longshoremen, and thousands of other artisans and laborers.

It would be misleading, however, to equate the New World's opportunity solely with its promise of material success. For many immigrants and native-born Americans, the glory of America lay in its social and political freedom. The absence of privileged classes, rigid castes, entrenched institutions, and political restrictions made Colonial America a land of opportunity in ways less tangible but no less meaningful than its chances for wealth—as the rise of Benjamin Franklin so clearly (if not so typically) portrays.

Even the system of indentured servitude provided opportunity. It permitted immigrants without any financial resources and of almost any age and skill to meet the high cost of an ocean-crossing by pledging their future labor. To their dismay, some indentured servants were purchased by cruel masters, some were assigned work incompatible with their talents, and others chafed under the confinements of temporary servitude. But for thousands of Europeans, the indenture system was an acceptable way to pay for a voyage that would eventually lead to a freehold or high wages and provide a chance to live as they pleased.

The selections presented here illustrate the views of some Colonial Americans toward the New World's varied opportunities. While most are optimistic, the last item in this section reflects the minority position: not for every colonist was the promise fulfilled.

6.—"EXCELLENT GOOD LAND"

Newcomers to America were struck by the ease and relatively low cost of acquiring land. Many, such as Robert Parke, an Irish Quaker in Delaware County, Pennsylvania, wrote the good tidings to relatives in Europe. This letter of 1725 from Parke to his sister in Ireland speaks primarily about land, but it also reveals much about life in the middle

colonies.—From Charles A. Hanna, The Scotch-Irish . . . *,*
and North America, *II (New York, 1902), pp. 64-67.*

CHESTER TOWNSHIP the — of the 10th Mo. 1725.

DEAR SISTER MARY VALENTINE:

This goes with a Salutation of Love to thee, Brother Thomas and
the children & in a word to all friends, Relations & well Wishers in
Generall as if named, hoping it may find you all in good health, as I
with all our family in Generall are in at this present writing & has
been since our arival, for we have not had a day's Sickness in the
Family Since we came into the Country, blessed be God for it. My
father in Particular has not had his health better these ten years than
Since he Came here, his ancient age considered. Our Irish Acquaintance in general are well Except Thoe: Lightfoot who Departed this
Life at Darby in a Good old age About 4 weeks Since. Thee writes
in thy Letter that there was a talk went back to Ireland that we were
not Satisfyed in coming here, which was Utterly false: now let this
Suffice to Convince you. In the first place he that carried back this
Story was an Idle fellow, & one of our Ship-Mates, but not thinking
this country Suitable to his Idleness, went back. . . . He is Sort of a
Lawyer, or Rather a Lyar as I may term him, therefore I wod not
have you give credit to Such false reports for the future, for there is
not one of the family but what likes the country very well & wod If
we were in Ireland again come here Directly it being the best country
for working folk & tradesmen of any in the world. But for Drunkards
and Idlers, they cannot live well any where. It is likewise an Extradin.
healthy country. . . . Land is of all Prices Even from ten Pounds,
to one hundred Pounds a hundred, according to the goodness or else
the situation thereof, & Grows dearer every year by Reason of Vast
Quantities of People that come here yearly from Several Parts of the
world, therefore thee & thy family or any that I wish well I wod
desire to make what Speed you can to come here the Sooner the
better. We have traveled over a Pretty deal of this country to seek
the Land, & [though] we met with many fine Tracts of Land here &
there in the country, yet my father being curious & somewhat hard
to Please Did not buy any Land until the Second day of 10th mo:
Last and then he bought a Tract of Land consisting of five hundred
Acres for which he gave 350 pounds. It is Excellent good land but
none cleared, Except about 20 Acres, with a small log house and
Orchard Planted, we are going to clear some of it Directly, for our

next Sumer's fallow. We might have bought Land much Cheaper but not so much to our Satisfaction. We stayed in Chester 3 months & then we Rented a Place 1 mile from Chester, with a good brick house & 200 Acres of Land for [—] pound a year, where we continue till next May. We have sowed about 200 Acres of wheat & 7 acres of rye this season. We sowed but a bushel on an acre, 3 pecks is Enough on new ground. I am grown an Experienced Plowman & my brother Abell is Learning. Jonathan & thy Son John drives for us. He is grown a Lusty fellow Since thou Saw him. We have the finest plows here that Can be. We plowed up our Sumer's fallows in May & June, with a Yoak of Oxen & 2 horses & they goe with as much Ease as Double the number in Ireland. We sow our wheat with 2 horses. A boy of 12 or 14 years old Can hold Plow here, a man Comonly holds & Drives himself. They plow an Acre, nay some Plows 2 Acres a day. They sow Wheat & Rye in August or September. We have had a crop of oats, barley & very good flax & hemp, Indian Corn & buckwheat all of our own Sowing & Planting this last summer. We also planted a bushel of white Potatoes Which Cost us 5 Shills. & we had 10 or 12 bushels Increase. This country yields Extraordinary Increase of all sorts of Grain Likewise—for nicholas hooper had of 3 Acres of Land & at most 3 bushels of Seed above 80 bushels Increase so that it is as Plentifull a Country as any Can be if people will be Industrious. . . . All Sorts of Provisions are Extraordinary Plenty in Philadelphia market, where Country people bring in their comodities. Their markets are on 4th day and 7th day. This country abounds in fruit, Scarce an house but has an Apple, Peach & cherry orchard. As for chestnuts, Wallnuts, & hasel nuts, Strawberrys, Billberrys & Mulberrys they grow wild in the woods and fields in Vast Quantities. They also make great Preperations against harvest; both Roast & boyled, Cakes & Tarts & Rum, stand at the Lands End, so that they may Eat and Drink at Pleasure. A Reaper has 2 Shills. & 3 pence a day, a mower has 2 Shills. & 6 pence & a pint of Rum beside meat & drink of the best; for no workman works without their Victuals in the bargain throughout the Country. A Laboring man has 18 or 20 pence a day in Winter. The Winters are not so cold as we Expected nor the Sumers so Extreme hot as formerly, for both Sumer and Winter are moderater than they ever were known. In Sumer time they wear nothing but a Shirt & Linnen drawers Trousers, which are breeches and stockings all in one made of Linnen; they are fine Cool wear in Sumer. As to what thee writt about the Governours Opening Letters it is Utterly false & nothing but a Lye

& any one Except bound Servants may go out of the Country when they will & Servants when they Serve their time may Come away If they please but it is rare any are such fools to leave the Country Except men's business require it. They pay 9 Pounds for their Passage (of this money) to go to Ireland. There is 2 fairs, yearly & 2 markets weekly in Philadephia also 2 fairs yearly in Chester & Likewise in new castle, but they Sell no Cattle nor horses, no living Creatures, but altogether Merchant's Goods, as hatts, Linnen & woolen Cloth, handkerchiefs, knives, Scizars, tapes & treds buckels, Ribonds & all Sorts of necessarys fit for our wooden Country & here all young men and women that wants wives or husbands may be Supplyed. Lett this Suffice for our fairs. As to meetings they are so plenty one may ride to their choice. I desire thee to bring or Send me a bottle of good Oyle fit for guns, thee may buy it in Dublin. . . . Dear Sister I wod not have thee Doupt the truth of what I write, for I know it to be true Tho I have not been long here. I wod have you Cloath yourselves well with Woolen & Linnen, Shoes & Stockings & hats for Such things are dear hear, & yet a man will Sooner Earn a suit of Cloths here than in Ireland, by Reason workman's Labour is so Dear. . . . I wod have you bring for your own Use 2 or 3 good falling Axes, a pair of beetle rings & 3 Iron wedges, for they are of good Service here. Your Plow Irons will not answer here, therefore you had better bring 1 or 2 hundred Iron. You may bring your Plow Chains as they are also a good —— Iron. . . . Dear Sister I desire thee may tell my old friend Samuel Thornton that he could give so much credit to my words & find no Iffs nor ands in my Letter, that in Plain terms he could not do better than to Come here, for both his & his wife's trade are Very good here. The best way for him to do is to pay what money he Can Conveniently Spare at that side & Engage himself to Pay the rest at this Side & when he Comes here if he Can get no friend to lay down the money for him, when it Comes to the worst, he may hire out 2 or 3 children. & I wod have him Cloath his family as well as his Small Ability will allow. Thee may tell him what things are proper to bring with him both for his Sea Store & for his Use in this Country. I wod have him Procure 3 or 4 Lusty Servants & Agree to pay their passage at this Side he might sell 2 & pay the others' passage with the money. I fear my good will to him will be of Little Effect by reason he is So hard of beleif, but thou mayest Assure him from me that if I had not a particular Respect for him & his family I Should not have writ so much for his Encouragement. . . .

7.—A FREE SOCIETY

*To many eighteenth-century immigrants, the social equality
of British America was as appealing as its economic prospects. While in every colony certain individuals and families enjoyed special prestige and privilege, the dominant
social pattern was remarkably egalitarian—though perhaps
not quite to the extent described by Hector St. John de
Crevecoeur in his* Letters from an American Farmer,
*written in the 1770s and published in 1782.—From Hector
St. John de Crevecoeur,* Letters from an American Farmer
(*New York, 1908*), *pp. 48-50, 72-76.*

I wish I could be acquainted with the feelings and thoughts which
must agitate the heart and present themselves to the mind of an
enlightened Englishman, when he first lands on this continent. He
must greatly rejoice that he lived at a time to see this fair country
discovered and settled; he must necessarily feel a share of national
pride, when he views the chain of settlements which embellishes these
extended shores. When he says to himself, this is the work of my
countrymen, who, when convulsed by factions, afflicted by a variety
of miseries and wants, restless and impatient, took refuge here. They
brought along with them their national genius, to which they prin-
cipally owe what liberty they enjoy, and what substance they possess.
Here he sees the industry of his native country displayed in a new
manner, and traces in their works the embrios of all the arts, sciences,
and ingenuity which flourish in Europe. Here he beholds fair cities,
substantial villages, extensive fields, an immense country filled with
decent houses, good roads, orchards, meadows, and bridges, where
an hundred years ago all was wild, woody and uncultivated! What
a train of pleasing ideas this fair spectacle must suggest; it is a prospect which must inspire a good citizen with the most heartfelt pleasure. The difficulty consists in the manner of viewing so extensive a
scene. He is arrived on a new continent; a modern society offers
itself to his contemplation, different from what he had hitherto seen.
It is not composed, as in Europe, of great lords who possess every
thing, and of a herd of people who have nothing. Here are no aristo-
cratical families, no courts, no kings, no bishops, no ecclesiastical

dominion, no invisible power giving to a few a very visible one; no great manufacturers employing thousands, no great refinements of luxury. The rich and the poor are not so far removed from each other as they are in Europe. Some few towns excepted, we are all tillers of the earth, from Nova Scotia to West Florida. We are a people of cultivators, scattered over an immense territory, communicating with each other by means of good roads and navigable rivers, united by the silken bands of mild government, all respecting the laws, without dreading their power, because they are equitable. We are all animated with the spirit of an industry which is unfettered and unrestrained, because each person works for himself. If he travels through our rural districts he views not the hostile castle, and the haughty mansion, contrasted with the clay-built hut and miserable cabbin, where cattle and men help to keep each other warm, and dwell in meanness, smoke, and indigence. A pleasing uniformity of decent competence appears throughout our habitations. The meanest of our log-houses is a dry and comfortable habitation. Lawyer or merchant are the fairest titles our towns afford; that of a farmer is the only appellation of the rural inhabitants of our country. It must take some time ere he can reconcile himself to our dictionary, which is but short in words of dignity, and names of honour. There, on a Sunday, he sees a congregation of respectable farmers and their wives, all clad in neat homespun, well mounted, or riding in their own humble waggons. There is not among them an esquire, saving the unlettered magistrate. There he sees a parson as simple as his flock, a farmer who does not riot on the labour of others. We have no princes, for whom we toil, starve, and bleed: we are the most perfect society now existing in the world. Here man is free as he ought to be. . . .

• • •

Europe contains hardly any other distinctions but lords and tenants; this fair country alone is settled by freeholders, the possessors of the soil they cultivate, members of the government they obey, and the framers of their own laws, by means of their representatives. This is a thought which you have taught me to cherish; our difference from Europe, far from diminishing, rather adds to our usefulness and consequence as men and subjects. Had our forefathers remained there, they would only have crouded it, and perhaps prolonged those convulsions which had shook it so long. Every industrious European who transports himself here, may be compared to a sprout growing at the foot of a great tree; it enjoys and draws but a little portion of sap; wrench it from the parent roots, transplant it, and it will become a tree bearing fruit also. Colonists are therefore entitled to the consideration due to the most useful subjects; a hundred families barely existing in some parts of Scotland, will here in six years, cause an annual exportation of 10,000 bushels of wheat: 100 bushels being but a common quantity for an industrious family to sell, if they cultivate good land. It is here then that the idle may be employed, the useless become useful, and the poor become rich; but by riches I do not mean gold and silver, we have but little of those metals; I mean a better sort of wealth, cleared lands, cattle, good houses, good cloaths, and an increase of people to enjoy them.

There is no wonder that this country has so many charms, and presents to Europeans so many temptations to remain in it. A traveller in Europe becomes a stranger as soon as he quits his own kingdom; but it is otherwise here. We know, properly speaking, no strangers; this is every person's country; the variety of our soils, situations, climates, governments, and produce, hath something which must please every body. No sooner does an European arrive, no matter of what condition, than his eyes are opened upon the fair prospect; he hears his language spoke, he retraces many of his own country manners, he perpetually hears the names of families and towns with which he is acquainted; he sees happiness and prosperity in all places disseminated; he meets with hospitality, kindness, and plenty every where; he beholds hardly any poor, he seldom hears of punishments and executions; and he wonders at the elegance of our towns, those miracles of industry and freedom. He cannot admire enough our rural districts, our convenient roads, good taverns, and our many accommodations; he involuntarily loves a country where every thing is so lovely. When in England, he was a mere Englishman; here he stands on a larger portion of the globe, not less than its fourth part, and may see the productions of the north, in iron and naval stores; the provisions of Ireland, the grain of Egypt, the indigo, the rice of China. He does not find, as in Europe, a crouded society, where every place is over-stocked; he does not feel that perpetual collision of parties, that difficulty of beginning, that contention which oversets so many. There is room for every body in America; has he any particular talent, or industry? he exerts it in order to procure a livelihood, and it succeeds. Is he a merchant? the avenues of trade are infinite; is he eminent in any respect? he will be employed and respected. Does he love a country life? pleasant farms present themselves; he may purchase what he wants, and thereby become an American farmer. Is he a labourer, sober and industrious? he need not go many miles, nor receive many informations before he will be hired, well fed at the table of his employer, and paid four or five times more than he can get in Europe. Does he want uncultivated lands? thousands of acres present themselves, which he may purchase cheap. Whatever be his talents or inclinations, if they are moderate, he may satisfy them. I do not mean that every one who comes will grow rich in a little time; no, but he may procure an easy, decent maintenance, by his industry. Instead of starving he will be fed, instead of being idle he will have employment; and these are riches enough for such men as come over here. The rich stay in Europe, it is only the middling and the poor that emigrate. Would you wish to travel in independent idleness, from north to south, you will find easy access, and the most chearful reception at every house; society without ostentation, good cheer without pride, and every decent diversion which the country affords, with little expence. It is no wonder that the European who has lived here a few years, is desirous to remain; Europe with all its pomp, is not to be compared to this continent, for men of middle stations, or labourers.

8.—A FLOURISHING COMMERCE

In 1740 Robert Dinwiddie, His Majesty's surveyor-general for the southern colonies (and later lieutenant-governor of Virginia), presented to the Board of Trade a detailed "Computation of the Value and Trade of the British Empire of America." It shows clearly that before the Revolution opportunity in America was not confined to the farm or plantation; it existed as well for men engaged in commerce and shipping.—From Documents Relating to the Colonial History of the State of New Jersey, *ed. William A. Whitehead, VI (Newark, 1882), pp. 83-91.*

To the Right honorable the LORDS COMMISSIONERS for TRADE and PLANTATIONS.

My Lords'
   I have been at a great deal of Trouble and Expence to inform Myself of the Trade of his Majesty's American Empire, and the annuall amount of the National Produce of each Colony or Plantation: I give You the following Thoughts, Observations and Calcula-

tions, which is partly from my own knowledge and from the best informations I possibly could get. . . .

• • •

First—Is [an] Account of the Vessels belonging to his Majestys Subjects in America distinguished by each Colony, beginning at Newfoundland and ending at Barbados

	Vessells
Belonging to Newfoundland,......................................	25
The Government of New England Vessells of different Denominations used in foreign Trade......................................	750
In the Same Government entirely employed in Fishing and Coasting being Sloops & Schooners......................................	350
In Connecticutt and Rhode Island in foreign Trade...................	260
In Ditto used in Fishing and Coasting Sloops and Schooners..........	150
In New York and Jerseys, in foreign Trade and in Coasting &c:.......	60
In Pensylvania and the lower Countys.............................	70
In Maryland..	60
In Virginia..	80
In North Carolina..	25
In South Carolina..	25
In Bermuda..	75
In Providence and Bahama Islands.................................	20
In Jamaica..	30
In Leeward and Virgin Islands....................................	35
In Barbados...	20
	2035

You'll Please to observe there is two thousand and thirty five Sail of Vessells of all Dimensions and Denominations, belonging to his Majesty's Subjects in America, which, I believe, is rather under than above the exact number, But must notice that upwards of five hundred of them are small and used in the Fishery and Coasting Trade, which will be noticed when we come to the Valuation of them.

Secondly—Here follows the Account from information of the Ships &c: Trading to and from America belonging to Great Britain and Ireland distinguished by the Trade they are concerned in.

	Vessells
To Newfoundland with the Fishermen and those employed in carrying Fish to the different Markets.................................	80
To New England and Nova Scotia.................................	20
To Connecticutt and Rhode Island.................................	6
To New York and the Jerseys.....................................	8

To Pensylvania... 10
To Maryland.. 95
To Virginia.. 120
To North Carolina... 30
To South Carolina.. 200
To Jamaica.. 100
To Leeward Islands... 151
To Barbados.. 80

———
900

Add to the above One hundred and fifty Sail from Great Britain and ⎱ 150
    Ireland to the Coast of Guinea, and so to the Plantations....... ⎰

———
1050
═══

Thirdly—An Estimate of the Value of the Vessels belonging to the Subjects of America, and Those belonging to Great Britain and Ireland Trading to the different Colonys &c:

1065—Ships, Snows [small sailing vessels] and Brigantines belonging to the American Subjects trading to foreign parts, valued at a medium £1000 Sterling each is.............	1,065,000
.970—Sloops and Schooners of smaller Size and Burthen, valued one with the other at £400 Sterling each is.............	.388,000
.900—Ships, Snows &c. from Great Britain and Ireland to and from the Plantations, valued at £1,200 each............	1,080,000
.150—Ditto from Great Britain and Ireland to the Coast of Guinea and the Plantations, with extraordinary Outfitts £1500 Each.......................................	225,000

———
3,085 Sail   £2,758,000

Fourthly—An Estimate of the Natural and Improved annuall Produce of his Majesty's American Colonys and Plantations, distinguished into each Colony or Plantation.

Newfoundland by Fish and Oyl.............................. £ 100,000
New England and Nova Scotia by Fish, Oyl, Whalebone, Cattle, Lumber Pitch, Tarr, Turpintine, Building of Vessels &c:...	800,000
Connecticutt and Rhode Island, with the same Commoditys and Sheep, Corn, Bread, Flour, Cheese and Butter.............	150,000
New York and the Jerseys with the same, and Tarr, Copper-Ore, Iron and Wheat.......................................	250,000
Pensylvania and the Lower Countys the Same & Tobacco......	280,000
Maryland, in the Same....................................	200,000
Virginia in the Same, with Pitch, Tarr, & Turpintine..........	250,000
North Carolina in the Same...............................	60,000

South Carolina in Ditto with Rice.............................	200,000
Bermuda, in Plett, Live-Stock, Fish, Oyl, Cabbage, Onions & Stones for building...	10,000
Bahama Islands in Salt, Timber, Plank, Barke, Turtle Shell, Brazilwood & Fruit......................................	15,000
Jamaica in Sugar, Mellasses, Rum, Cotton, Limejuice, Ginger, Indico, Coffee, Alloes, Piemento, Turtle Shell, Mahogany Timber, and Plank......................................	500,000
Antigua in the Same Commoditys.............................	250,000
St. Christophers......in Ditto...............................	220,000
Nevis...............in Ditto..............................	50,000
Mountserratt.........in Ditto..............................	50,000
Auguilla.............in Ditto..............................	15,000
Tortola.............in Ditto..............................	30,000
Spanish Town........in Ditto..............................	15,000
Barbados............in Ditto..............................	300,000
	3,745,000
Fifthly—The Amount of the Value of Goods Shipped from Great Britain and Ireland to our British Plantations and the Coast of Guinea is annually by Computation....................	2,550,000
Sixthly—A Calculation of the amount of Cash, Dye Woods, Druggs, Cocoa, &c. imported to the British Plantations, being the consequence of a Trade carried on to Spanish and French Dominions in America. That Trade in New England, Connecticutt and Rhode Island in Dye Woods from Honduras, Some Cash and Cacao amounts to yearly...........	100,000
To New York (circa)..	25,000
To Bermuda...	10,000
To Jamaica..	250,000
To Leeward Islands (circa)...................................	20,000
To Barbados (circa)..	20,000
	£425,000

It's to be observed that as this is the Produce of foreign Colony's, it's mentioned by itself, to Shew the amount of that private Branch of Trade, and tho' it's carried on with Goods from Britain and Negroes, which is before considered in the Calculate, yet it's conceived, that the addition of this will not over Rate our American Trade.

Seventhly—The whole brought into an Account by which You may See the Amount of the above American Trade.

The amount of the computed Value of the Vessells trading in America, including those belonging to the Merchants of Great Britain and Ireland being 3085, which amounts to.........	2,758,000
The Amount of the Natural and Improved Produce of the British Colonys, which employ the above Vessells................	3,745,000
The amount of Goods from Great Britain and Ireland to the Plantations and Coast of Guinea annually................	2,550,000
The Amount of a Casual Trade carried on to the Spanish and French Settlements in America annually (circa)............	425,000
	£9,478,000

You will please to observe that the whole Trade to and in America, belonging to his Majesty's British and American Subjects (Hudson's Bay only excepted) amounts yearly to Nine Million four hundred and seventy eight thousand pounds; This includes the Value of the whole Navigation, the annual Supplys from Great Britain and Ireland, the Naturall and Improved Produce remitted to Europe from the Plantations and Colonys, as well as the Supplys given each other by their Traffick and Commerce from one Colony or Plantation to the Other. . . .

• • •

Upon the foregoing Observations and Calculations, I believe, You will think that the British Empire of America is of inestimable value to the Nation of Great Britain. Please to observe the Trade and Fishery of America, abstract of Hudson's Bay, employs 3,085 Sail of Vessells of different Denominations and Burthen; allowing eight Men to navigate each Vessell, there is employ'd in that Trade only; 24,680 Mariners, which I think is a fine Nursery for our Sailors.

As for the Revenue arising from the American Trade, I must referr to those that are acquainted with the Receipts thereof.

If the foregoing be acceptable and agreeable to You, it fully answers my intent; if any Errors in the Calculations, its wholly owing to my Informations, tho' I have reason to think it's pretty Just; but that and the whole is entirely submitted to your Superior Judgment, and I always am with Gratitude and Duty

    Your Lordships Most Obedient Humble Servant
    London April 1740   Robert Dinwiddie

9.—THE BENEFITS
OF TEMPORARY SERVITUDE

Throughout the eighteenth century the majority of Amer-
ica's immigrants came as indentured servants, paying their
passage by working several years for whoever reimbursed
the shipowner or his agent. By this method Colonial Amer-
ica gained not only laborers and craftsmen, but professional
people as well—as is illustrated by the account of John
Harrower, a schoolteacher.—From John Harrower, "Diary,
1773-1776," American Historical Review, *VI (1900-1901),*
pp. 67, 70-72, 75-79, 82-84, 91.

Monday, 6th December 1773. This morning I left my house [on
Shetland Island] and family at 4 OClock in order to travel in search
of business. . . .

• • •

[*Tuesday*], *18th* [*January 1774*]. This day I got to London and
was like a blind man without a guide, not knowing where to go being
freindless and having no more money but fifteen shillings and eight
pence farthing a small sum to enter London with; But I trust in the
mercys of God who is a rich provider and am hopefull before it is
done some way will cast up for me. I took up my lodging at the old
ship Tavern in little Hermitage street, Mr. George Newton being the
landlord, but in Prison for debt at present.

Wednesday, 19th. This day I shifted my cloaths and put on a
clean Ruffled Shirt, clean Britches and waistcoat and my Brown Coat,
I not having any other cloaths on ever since I left Lerwick but my
blew Jacket and Bigg Coat above it and a plain shirt. At 11 AM I
called to see Capt. Perry, but was told he would not be at home
untill 5 pm. Having eat nothing for 24 houres, I dinned in my Lodging this day which cost me 1/2 Sterling. After dinner I took a walk
with the mate of a ship a Scotsman who carried me through Virginia
street, London street, part of White Chappel street, down to London
Hospitall, through Ragg fair, the Minnories, Round Tour hill, and
the Tour, through Saint Catharins, and Bur street and so home.

A 5 pm called again at Capt. Perrys and the first face I saw was

Willie Holcraw of Coningsburgh who I found staid here as a servant, and while I was speacking to him, Capt. Perry came home and he immediatly knew me, and desired me to walk in which I did, and after sitting some time and drinking some tea, I called Capt. Perry aside and made my Intentions known to him, at same time begged his advice and assistance; He told me he hardly thought there would be any Business got for me in London. But told me to call on him at the Jamaica Coffee House to morrow at Change time. I then went home. and soon went to Bedd.

Thursday, 20th. This morning breackfast at home and paid 6d. for it. At noon called at the Jamaica Coffee House and soon after seed Capt. Perry and waited here and Change untill 3 pm but no appearance of any Business for me. the time I was in the Coffee house I drank 3ds. worth of punch, and I was obliged to make it serve me for Dinner. at night I hade ½d. worth of bread and 1d. of Cheese and a poynt of Porter for supper it being all I cou'd afford.

Freiday, 21st. This morning I seed an advertisement for Book-[k]eepers and Clerks to go to a Gentlemen [at] Philadelphia. I went as it directed to No. 1 in Catharine Court princes street, but when I came there I was told they were served. I then waited again on Capt. Perry untill after 3 pm But to no purpose. I this day offered to go steward of a ship bound to Maryland but could not get the birth. This day I was 3 or 4 miles through London and seed St. Paul's Church, the Bank of England where I seed the gold lying in heaps, I also seed Summerst house, Gild hall, Drury Lane, Covingarden, Adelphus Buildings and several other pleaces. I then returnd and near my lodgings I dinned at an eating house and hade 4d. worth of roast Beiff 1d. worth of bread and a poynt of small beer, in all 5½d.

Saturday, 22d. This morning I seed an advertisement in the Publick ledger for a Messenger to a publick Lodge, Sallery 15/ Sterling per week and another advertisement for an under Clerk to a Merchant to both which I wrote answers and went to the places apointed, and found at each place more than a dozen of Letters before me, so that I had litle expectation that way they being all weel aquanted and I a stranger. I then went to change to see if any thing would cas[t] up but to no purpose, so I returned hom at 4 pm and spent the evening in a verry sollitary manner supping on bread and Cheese as usuall.

•   •   •

Wednesday, 26th. This day I being reduced to the last shilling I hade was obliged to engage to go to Virginia for four years as a schoolmaster for Bedd, Board, washing and five pound during the

whole time. . . . At 3 pm this day I went on board the Snow Planter
Capt. Bowers Commissioner for Virginia now lying at Ratliff Cross,
and imediatly as I came on board I received my Hammock and
Bedding. . . .

Thursday, 27th. This day ranie weather. the ships crew imployed
in rigging the ship under the Direction of the mate and I was imployed in getting my Hammock slung. at 2 pm came on board Alexander Burnet nephew to Mr. Francis Farquharson writter in Edinburgh and one Samuel Mitchell a Cooper from Yorkshire and both
entred into the berth and Mace [mess] with Stewart and me.

Saturday, 29th. This day came on board Alexander Kennedy a
young man from Edinburgh who hade been a Master Cooper there
and a Glasgow Man by trade a Barber both which we took into our
Mace, which compleated it being five Scotsmen and one Yorkshire-
man, and was always called the Scots mace, And the Capt. told me
he was from the Toun of Aberbothick in Scotland, but that he [had]
not been there since he was fifteen years of age but hade been always
in the Virginia trade which I was verry glad to hear.

Munday, 31st. This day I went ashore and bought a penknife, a
paper Book, and some paper and pens and came on board to Dinner.
It is surprising to see the No. of good tradesmen of all kinds, that
come on board every day.

Freiday, February 4th. This day at 7 AM unmoored from Rat-
liffcross and fell down the river with the tide there being no wind. . . .

• • •

Thursday, 28th [*April*]. At 7 AM the Pillot wegh'd Anchor and
wrought the ship up to Hampton Roads where we came to an Anchor
at 10 A M. This morning I was employ'd in Making out a Clean list
of the servants names and Business and age, and how soon I was
done Capt. Bowers went ashore in the Pillot boat to Hamton on
Elizabeth river. . . .

Monday, May 2d. . . . At 2 p.m. the Capt. Carried five servants
ashore to Hampton in order to sell their Indentures, But returned again at Midnight with[out] selling any more but one Boat
Builder. . . .

• • •

Tuesday, 10th. At 2 A M weighed and stood up with the tide,
came to an anchor at 6 A M and lay untill Ditto 8 when we weighed
with a fair wind and got to our Moorings at 6 pm at the Toun of
Fredericksburgh. . . .

• • •

Munday, 16th. This day severalls came on board to purchase servants Indentures and among them there was two Soul drivers. they are men who make it their business to go on board all ships who have in either Servants or Convicts and buy sometimes the whole and sometimes a parcell of them as they can agree, and then they drive them through the Country like a parcell of Sheep untill they can sell them to advantage, but all went away without buying any.

Tuesday, 17th. This day Mr. Anderson the Merchant sent for me into the [cabin] and verry genteely told me that on my recomendations he would do his outmost to get me settled as a Clerk or bookeeper if not as a schoolmaster which last he told me he thought wou'd turn out more to my advantage upon being settled in a good famely.

The ships crew and servants employed in getting ashore all the cask out of the hould, no sales this day.

Wednesday, 18th. This day the ships crew and servants imployed in getting out the ballast and unrigging the ship. One Cooper, one Blacksmith and one Shoemaker were settled with Masters this day.

Thursday, 19th. One Farmer's time sold and one Cabinet Maker on tryall.

Saturday, 21st. This day one Mr. Cowly a man 'twixt fifty and sixty years of age, a servant, also three sons of his their ages from eight to fourteen were all settled with one McDonald a Scotchman.

Munday, 23d. This morning a great number of Gentlemen and Ladies driving into Town it being an annuall Fair day and tomorrow the day of the Horse races. at 11 A M Mr. Anderson begged to settle as a schoolmaster with a friend of his one Colonel Daingerfield and told me he was to be in Town tomorrow, or perhaps tonight, and how soon he came he shou'd aquant me. at same time all the rest of the servants were ordred ashore to a tent at Fredericksburg and severall of their Indentures were then sold. about 4 pm I was brought to Colonel Daingerfield, when we imediatly agreed and my Indenture for four years was then delivered him and he was to send for me the next day. at same time ordred to get all my dirty Cloaths of every kind washed at his expense in Toun; at night he sent me five shillings on board by Capt. Bowers to keep my pocket.

Tuesday, 24th. This morning I left the Ship at 6 A M having been sixteen weeks and six days on board her. . . .

Wednesday, 25th. I lodged in a Tavern last night and paid 7½ for my Bedd and 7½ for my breackfast. this morning a verry heavy rain untill 11 A M. Then I received my Linens &c. all clean washed and packing every thing up I went onboard the ship and Bought this Book for which I paid 18d. Sterling. I also bought a small Divinity book called the Christian Monitor and a spelling book, both at 7½ and an Arithmetick at 1/6d. all for my Account.

Thursday, 26th. This day at noon the Colonel sent a Black with a cuple of Horses for me and soon after I set out on Horseback and aravied at his seat of Belvidera about 3 pm and after I hade dined the Colonel took me to a neat little house at the upper end of an Avenue of planting at 500 yards from the Main house, where I was to keep the school, and Lodge myself in it.

This place is verry pleasantly situated on the Banks of the River Rappahannock about seven miles below the Toun of Fredericksburgh and the school's right above the Warff so that I can stand in the door and pitch a stone onboard of any ship or Boat going up or coming doun the river.

Freiday, 27th. This morning about 8 A M the Colonel delivered his three sons to my Charge to teach them to read write and figure. his oldest son Edwin 10 years of age, intred into two syllables in the spelling book, Bathourest [Bathurst] his second son six years of age in the Alphabete and William his third son 4 years of age does not know the letters. he has likeways a Daughter whose name is Hanna Bassett — Years of age. Soon after we were all sent for to breackfast to which we hade tea, Bread, Butter and cold meat and there was at table the Colonel, his Lady, his Children, the housekeeper and myself. At 11 A M the Colonel and his Lady went some where to pay a visite, he upon horseback and she in her Charriot. At 2 pm I dined with the Housekeeper the Children and a stranger Lady. at 6 pm I left school, and then I eat plenty of fine strawberries, but they neither drink Tea in the afternoon nor eat any supper here for the most part. My school Houres is from 6 to 8 in the morning, in the forenoon from 9 to 12 and from 3 to 6 in the afternoon.

•　　•　　•

Sunday, August 7th. This afternoon meeting accidentaly with a Gentleman here who was on his way to London I wrote my wife a few lines by him having wrote her fully 14th June last but having omitted to insert the Coppy in it's proper place I now do it here before I insert the coppy of my second Letter to her from this country.

BELVIDERA 14th June 1774.

My Dearest Life

I wrote you from London on Wednesday 26th. Jan. last which Im hopefull came safe to hand, and found you and my dear Infants in perfect health, and am hopefull this will find both you and them in the same state, As I am at present and have been I bless God since I left you. You will remember when I wrote you last, I informed you that I was to go for Baltimore in Maryland, But I altred my design in that and came here it being a more healthy pleace. I sailed from London on Freiday the 4th. Feb. last, and arrived in Hampton roads in Virginia on the 27 April, having been a Month of the time at Spithead in England. As to particulars of our Voyage &c. it would take up too much room here to insert it. But I have a Journal of every days transactions and remarcable Occurances since the morning I left you which will be amusing to you when please God we are spared to meet, for I design to see and prepare a way for you all in this Country how soon I am able.—I shall now aquant you with my situation in this Country. I am now settled with on[e] Colonel W. Dangerfield Esq of Belvidera, on the Banks of the River Rappahannock about 160 miles from the Capes or sea mouth, and seven Miles below the Toun of Fredericksburgh. My business is to teach his Children to read write and figure, Edwin his oldest son about 8 years of [age] Bathurest his second 6 years of age and William his youngest son 4 years of age. he has also a Daughter whose name is Hanna Basset. I came to this place on Thursday 26th May and next morning I received his three sons into my charge to teach, the two youngest boys I got in A : B : C. and the oldest Just begun to syllab and I have now the two youngest spelling and the oldest reading. I am obliged to teach in the English method which was a little aquard to me at first but now quite easy. I am also obliged to talk english the best I can, for Lady Dangerfield speacks nothing but high english, and the Colonel hade his Education in England and is a verry smart Man. As to my agreement it is as follows Viz. I am obliged to continue with Col. Dangerfield for four years if he insists on it, and for teaching his own children I have Bed, Board, washing and all kind of Cloaths during the above time, and for what scholars I can get more than his Children I have five shillings curency per Quarter for each of them, which is equall to four shillings sterling, and I expect ten or twelve to school next week, for after I hade been here eight days and my abilities and my behavior sufficiently tried, the Colonel rode through the neighbouring Gentlemen and Planters in order to procure scollars for me, so that I hope in a short time to make something of it. And as I have no Occasion to spend a farthing on myself every shilling I make shall be carefully remitted you, for your support and my Dear Infants. But I must be some time here before any thing can be done. . . .

. . . My school is a neate litle House 20 foot long and 12 foot wide and it stands by itself at the end of an Avenue of planting about as far from the main house as Robt. Forbes's is from the burn, and there comes a bonny black bairn every morning to clean it out and make my bed, for I sleep in it by myself. I have a verry fine feather bed under me, and a pair of sheets, a thin fold of a Blanket and a Cotton bed spread is all my bed cloaths, and I find them just enough. as for myself I supose you wou'd scarce know me now, there being nothing either brown, blew, or black about me but the head and feet, I being Dressed in short cloath Coat, vest Coat, and britches all made of white cotton without any lyning and thread stockins and wearing my own hair curled round like a wigg. at present a suite of Cloaths costs five and twenty shillings here of making which I really think verry high.

·   ·   ·

I yet hope please God, if I am spared, some time to make you a Virginian Lady among the woods of America which is by far more pleasent than the roaring of the raging seas round abo't Zetland, And yet to make you eat more wheat Bread in your old age than what you have done in your Youth. But this I must do by carefullness, industry and a Close Application to Business, which ye may take notice of in this letter I am doing Sunday as well as Saturday nor will I slip an honest method nor an hour whereby I can gain a penny for yours and my own advantage.

10.—THE DARKER SIDE

For some colonists, especially indentured servants, America turned out to be more a land of misery than of opportunity. In the selections that follow, Gottlieb Mittelberger portrays the plight of some Germans who arrived in Pennsylvania; selections from contemporary newspapers have been added at the end of his account to illustrate the chronic problem of runaway servants. Of course it cannot be known from the newspaper advertisements whether the master had mis-used his servant or the servant was irresponsibly violating the terms of indenture. In either event, the prevalence of runaway servants reflected deep dissatisfactions within colonial society.—From Gottlieb Mittelberger's Journey to Pennsylvania in the Year 1750 . . . , *tr. Carl T. Eben*

*(Philadelphia, 1898), pp. 25-29; and from originals and
photocopies of colonial newspapers at Columbia University
and The New-York Historical Society.*

When the ships have landed at Philadelphia after their long voyage, no one is permitted to leave them except those who pay for their passage or can give good security; the others, who cannot pay, must remain on board the ships till they are purchased, and are released from the ships by their purchasers. The sick always fare the worst, for the healthy are naturally preferred and purchased first; and so the sick and wretched must often remain on board in front of the city for 2 or 3 weeks, and frequently die, whereas many a one, if he could pay his debt and were permitted to leave the ship immediately, might recover and remain alive.

• • •

The sale of human beings in the market on board the ship is carried on thus: Every day Englishmen, Dutchmen and High-German people come from the city of Philadelphia and other places, in part from a great distance, say 20, 30, or 40 hours away, and go on board the newly arrived ship that has brought and offers for sale passengers from Europe, and select among the healthy persons such as they deem suitable for their business, and bargain with them how long they will serve for their passage-money, which most of them are still in debt for. When they have come to an agreement, it happens that adult persons bind themselves in writing to serve 3, 4, 5 or 6 years for the amount due by them, according to their age and strength. But very young people, from 10 to 15 years, must serve till they are 21 years old.

Many parents must sell and trade away their children like so many head of cattle; for if their children take the debt upon themselves, the parents can leave the ship free and unrestrained; but as the parents often do not know where and to what people their children are going, it often happens that such parents and children, after leaving the ship, do not see each other again for many years, perhaps no more in all their lives.

When people arrive who cannot make themselves free, but have children under 5 years, the parents cannot free themselves by them; for such children must be given to somebody without compensation to be brought up, and they must serve for their bringing up till they are 21 years old. Children from 5 to 10 years, who pay half price for their passage, viz. 30 florins, must likewise serve for it till they are 21 years of age; they cannot, therefore, redeem their parents by taking the debt of the latter upon themselves. But children above 10 years can take part of their parents' debt upon themselves.

A woman must stand for her husband if he arrives sick, and in like manner a man for his sick wife, and take the debt upon herself or himself, and thus serve 5 to 6 years not alone for his or her own debt, but also for that of the sick husband or wife. But if both are sick, such persons are sent from the ship to the sick-house [hospital], but not until it appears probable that they will find no purchasers. As soon as they are well again they must serve for their passage, or pay if they have means.

It often happens that whole families, husband, wife, and children, are separated by being sold to different purchasers, especially when they have not paid any part of their passage money.

When a husband or wife has died at sea, when the ship has made more than half of her trip, the survivor must pay or serve not only for himself or herself, but also for the deceased.

When both parents have died over half-way at sea, their children, especially when they are young and have nothing to pawn or to pay, must stand for their own and their parents' passage, and serve till they are 21 years old. When one has served his or her term, he or she is entitled to a new suit of clothes at parting; and if it has been so stipulated, a man gets in addition a horse, a woman, a cow.

When a serf has an opportunity to marry in this country, he or she must pay for each year which he or she would have yet to serve, 5 to 6 pounds. But many a one who has thus purchased and paid for his bride, has subsequently repented his bargain, so that he would gladly have returned his exorbitantly dear ware, and lost the money besides.

If some one in this country runs away from his master, who has treated him harshly, he cannot get far. Good provision has been made for such cases, so that a runaway is soon recovered. He who detains or returns a deserter receives a good reward.

If such a runaway has been away from his master one day, he must serve for it as a punishment a week, for a week a month, and for a month half a year. But if the master will not keep the runaway after he has got him back, he may sell him for so many years as he would have to serve him yet.

Work and labor in this new and wild land are very hard and manifold, and many a one who came there in his old age must work very hard to his end for his bread. . . .

[*The Runaways*]

[From the *Boston Evening Post,* July 11, 1748]

Ran away from his Master, *James Powner,* about 19 Years of Age, he is a stout lusty Fellow, with light coloured short Hair, something Pock-broken, his left Foot has been cut, so that his great Toe falls down He had on when he ran away, a striped Woollen Jacket, a striped Woollen Shirt, and a pair of old Ozenbrigs Trowsers. Whosoever shall take up the said Run-away, and convey him to his Master *Nathaniel Noyes* of *Falmouth* in *New Casco,* shall have *Five Pounds,* old Tenor,* Reward, and all necessary Charges paid.

Falmouth, June 30, 1748   *Nathaniel Noyes.*

Ran away from his Master *Benjamin Bacon* of *Salem,* Wig-maker, *June* the 10th. his Apprentice Boy, *Samuel Dove,* aged 12 Years, who wears light coloured short Hair, having on when he went away, striped Jacket and Breeches, a check'd Shirt, and a Felt Hat. Whoever shall take up the abovesaid Runaway, and bring him to his said Master, shall have *Three Pounds,* Old Tenor, Reward, and all necessary Charges paid

per me   *Benjamin Bacon.*

[From the *Pennsylvania Gazette,* August 2, 1759]

Germantown, July 18, 1759

Run away on the 13*th of this Instant, at Night, from the Subscriber, of said Town, an Apprentice Lad, named Stophel, or Christopher Hergesheimer, about* 19 *Years of Age, by Trade a Blacksmith, middle sized of his Age, has a sour down-looking Countenance, is of Dutch Extraction, but can talk good English; Had on, and took with him, when he went away, a bluish Cloath Coat, green Nap Jacket, Snuff coloured Breeches, and Linen Jacket and Breeches, all about half wore, two pair of Ozenbrigs Trowsers, two Ditto Shirts, and one pretty fine, a Pair of old Shoes, a Pair of Thread, and a Pair of Cot-*

---

* The first issue of Massachusetts paper money—ED.

ton *Stockings, a good Athlone Felt Hat, and yellowish Silk Hand-*
kerchief, wore his own dark brown short Hair, but may cut it off:
He had a Hurt on the Inside of his Left-hand, not quite cured, at
his going away. Whoever takes him up, and brings or conveys him
to his Master, or secures him in the Jail of Philadelphia, shall have
Forty Shillings Reward, and reasonable Charges, paid by

Matthew Potter, *junior.*

Lancaster County, July 24, 1759

Run away an Irish Servant Man, named Valentine Bullard, about
25 Years of Age, about five Feet seven Inches High, of a sandy Com-
plexion, wears his own Hair, marked with the Smallpox: Had on
when he went away, a home made brown Cloth Coat, a good new
Hat, one Shirt, one Pair of large cross barred Check Trowsers and
one Pair of Tow Ditto, and a Pair of strong Shoes. Whoever takes
up said Servant, and secures him in any Goal, so that his Master can
have him again, shall have Forty Shillings Reward, and reasonable
Charges, paid by

Peter Grubb.

Run away from the Subscriber, in Kent County Maryland, on the
9th of this Instant July, a Molattoe Servant Man, named Thomas
Williams, about 5 Feet 8 or 10 Inches high, is a strong, able, well
made Man, his Cloaths uncertain; he had about Thirty Pounds Cash
with him, and also his Wife, who is of his own Colour, and has a
great Impediment in her Speech. It is supposed they went to Virginia
in a Shallop. Whoever takes up the said Runaway and secures him
so that his Master gets him again, shall have Fifteen Pistoles Reward,
and Eight Pistoles for discovering the Person that carried him away,
so that he may be convicted thereof according to Law.

John Bordley

Philadelphia, March 3, 1759

Run away from the Subscriber, in St. Mary's County, Maryland, on
the 18th of February last, an Irish Convict Servant Man, named
Francis Erwin, a likely, well made, sly, insinuating Fellow, about six
Feet high, discovers his Country by his Tongue; he has a large Scar
on his Throat, and a Wheezing in his Speech: It is supposed he will

endeavour to pass for one Stephen Stiffert, having stole his Indenture with a Discharge thereon; he is a Blacksmith by Trade: Had on a dark brown bob Wig, a light coloured Duffil Coat, with flat Metal Buttons, a blue Halfthick Waistcoat and Breeches, with Buttons of the same Sort, but is supposed to have stolen other Clothes, and may change his Apparel as it suits his Conveniency. He rode off on a large bay Horse, shod all round, with a light hunting Saddle, half worn, without a Saddle-cloth, one of the Stirrups Iron, the other Brass, in Company with one Peter Turley, an Irishman, and is supposed to be gone to Philadelphia or New-York. Whoever takes up the said Servant, and secures him so that his Master may have him again, shall receive (besides what the Law allows) Four Pistoles, if taken in Maryland, Six if taken in Pennsylvania, and Eight if taken in New-York.

George Plater.

Run away from the Subscriber, living in this City, a Servant Man, named Charles Crouch, is about 25 Years of Age, Carolina born, about 5 Feet 10 Inches high, by Trade a Printer, wears his own black curl'd Hair, mostly tied behind, affects much of the Beau and Gamester, and is much inclin'd to Drink: Had on when he went away, an old olive colour'd Thickset Coat, black Allopeen Jacket, white Linen Shirt, black Breeches, white rib'd Stockings, and old Shoes. Whoever takes up said Servant, and secures him in any Goal, so that his Master may have him again, shall have THREE POUNDS Reward, and reasonable Charges, paid by

W. Dunlap

N. B.   *All Persons are forbid to harbour said Servant, as they may expect to be proceeded against to the utmost Rigour of the Law.*

❧

[From the *Pennsylvania Packet and General Advertiser,* November 16, 1772]

Baltimore County, *Maryland, Oct. 26th,* 1772.

TEN POUNDS REWARD

Ran away from the Subscriber, two convict servant men, viz. THOMAS WHEATLEY, about five feet eight or nine inches high, strait limbed, small featured, sandy hair and beard, with double teeth, and about 27 years of age: Had on a brown coat, white drab breeches, and pumps. The other named DANIEL UNTHANK, near the same height, about 20 years of age, has a fair smooth face, light brown hair, no beard, or very little. He took from me a great coat, of fine cloth, dove colour, basket buttons, small wooden buttons to the cape, moth-eaten in the back under the cape, and one pair of double soaled shoes. Both of them had fine shirts and felt hats. As they have some money, it is likely they will change their clothes. Whoever takes up and secures said servants in any goal, so that their master may have them again, shall have the above reward, paid by

AQUILA PRICE.

Philadelphia, November 16, 1772.

FIVE POUNDS REWARD.

Ran away from on board the ship Wolfe, Richard Hunter, master, from Londonderry, a redemptioner named COLLIN MCDONALD, born in the Highlands of Scotland, and will be easily known by his accent; about 36 years of age, a taylor by trade, about six feet high, with black short hair; had on a blue coat and red waistcoat; said he had a wife near Albany, and is supposed to have gone that way. Whoever apprehends the same, and brings him to the subscribers, shall have THREE POUNDS reward, if taken in this province, and if out of it, shall be entitled to the above reward, and all reasonable charges, paid by

GRAY, FLETCHER, and CO.

❧

[From *The New York Gazette or Weekly Post-Boy,* February 4, 1754]

Run away the 25th of December *last, from* John Scot, *of Hanover Township, Morris County, and Province of* New-Jersey, *a Servant Man named* James Murphy, *about 5 Feet 3 Inches high, much pitted with the Small-Pox, long yellow Hair tyed behind; he has been a Soldier in the* French *Service, talks good* French. *Served with said* Scott, *as a School-Master; had on when he went away a new Bearskine Coat with broad Hair Buttons, a light Colour'd Rateen Jacket, Check Shirt, and Leather Breeches; new Worsted Stockings, and new Pumps. Whoever secures said Servant, so as his Master may have him again, shall have* Forty Shillings *Reward and reasonable Charges paid by me*

JOHN SCOTT.

N. B.   *All Masters of Vessels are discharged on their Peril, from carrying him off.*

III

Patterns
of Settlement

Colonial America offered its inhabitants several modes of settlement. Some colonists chose to make their homes in the cities where jobs were plentiful; for the rest there was abundant land along the coast and in the fertile farm areas inland. For those who could not meet the rising cost of surveyed land, the back country beckoned with a promise of cheap land and an unfettered life.

Nine out of ten free Americans chose to make their homes in open farm country or in small clusters around a county courthouse or village church. From New Hampshire to Georgia most Americans avoided both the extreme isolation and danger of the frontier and the excessive clamor and congestion of the city. Thus pre-Revolutionary America remained predominantly a land of small towns and small farms, differing only in location and economic habits.

But the majority did not speak for all. On the western fringe of every colony (save the few which had no western claims) lived families whose urge for adventure or cheap land or greater freedom had led them away from the settled areas into the wilderness. Meanwhile, other Americans crowded into the few colonial cities, causing dramatic urban growth. Philadelphia had a population of 10,500 in 1725; by 1775 it had swelled to 40,000. In the same period New York grew from 7,500 to 25,000; Charleston from 4,000 to 12,000; and Newport from 4,200 to 11,000. Only Boston among the major cities failed to make marked gains during the half century before the Revolutionary War: its population of 12,500 in 1725 had grown to only 16,000 in 1775—largely because of its cramped peninsular location. Yet other than the five or six leading cities, there were few population centers of any note. On the eve of the Revolution several colonies were without a single town of more than 5,000 persons.

The War for Independence and the subsequent career of the new republic eventually caused rapid changes in America's demographic pattern. But in the half century before 1776 Colonial America knew only growth—in cities, towns, plantations, and farms, as well as along the western frontier.

11.—NORTHERN TOWNS
AND COUNTRYSIDE

In New England especially, but also in much of New York, New Jersey, Pennsylvania, and Delaware, settlement centered on small towns—although by the eighteenth century many farmers lived several miles from the village common. The first account below, by an English visitor, describes the pattern of settlement in the seaboard areas near Boston, Massachusetts. The second describes a thriving New England town—Portsmouth, New Hampshire—which boasted a population of perhaps 4,000 at the time James Birket visited there in 1750.—From Philip Padelford, ed., Colonial Panorama, 1775: Dr. Robert Honyman's Journal for March and April *(San Marino, Calif., 1939), pp. 45-49; and from James Birket,* Some Cursory Remarks Made by James Birket in His Voyage to North America, 1750-1751 *(New Haven, 1916), pp. 8-10.*

[Honyman]

23 March [1775]. Rose, dressed & breakfasted this morning as usual; after breakfast went down to the north end to Charlestown ferry, crost over to Charlestown, ferryage, one Copper. Hired a horse there, & a little before 12 set off for Salem, which is 20 miles distant. a pleasant day, though cold.—The country for 4 miles & a half till one comes to Mistick is well cultivated, being entirely cleared & enclosed with Stone fences, as is the case all through this Province. It is divided into large fields cheifly pasture, & is not remarkably hilly or rocky. Mistick is a village lying on the Top of a creek which runs into Boston harbour. It has a Meeting house with a Liberty Pole, & the same may be said of all the great & small towns in this Government. The meeting houses are large & neat with a number of good Windows & commonly with a very handsome steeple. Within a mile or two of Mistick, two rows of rocky hills on each side approach one another, & the road soon enters among them, & now there is a constant succession of rocky hills, & small Vallies till within about 7 miles of Salem. The Vallies seem to be good soil, fruitful & well cultivated. The Houses are most remarkably thick planted, very neat, & good looking people & cattle. Dined about 7 miles from Salem in Lynn township, & from thence to Salem the Country is little better than a rocky, bare & frightful desert, with Patches of soil here & there which are cultivated every foot of them, & the fences are even extended over the bare rocks. The houses are still frequent, & the road for half a mile from Salem is almost one continued street. The Country indeed mends a little to the northward of Salem. The roads as may easily be imagined are excessively bad, & from the nature of the ground, almost impossible to mend them.

Salem is a very large handsome town situated on a plain, larger in my opinion than Norfolk in Virginia. It consists of one main street of a vast length, one or two smaller ones parallel to it, & several cross Lanes. It has three meeting houses & an Episcopal church. It is a place of very great trade, chiefly in the fishing way, in oil & to the W. Indies. There are some of the longest & finest Rope walks & spinning houses I ever saw, & they were very busy in all of them making large ropes & cables. The Harbour & road were full of shipping, by far the greatest part of which were sloops & schooners. A branch of the Harbour runs up on the north side of the town, & over the upper part of this is the draw bridge. . . . The harbour lies on the South side of the town, is very narrow & seems very safe, & farther out is a large road, secured from the sea by several islands lying before it.—Arrived at Salem about 4 o'clock. Drank coffee & walked round the town. Went into a Church, where they were holding a town meeting; the matter under consideration was the forming & training an Artillery company, & one of the leading men offered to make a present of two pieces of Cannon to the town.

About 6 set off for Marble head, which is 4 miles from Salem, & the Steeples of Marble head may be seen from Salem. The road is pretty good, considering the rocky country it passes through, almost entirely bare of earth, & yet here along the road are many good houses. Past over a bridge at the head of a branch of the road of Salem which runs up a long way to the Southward of the Town. Arrived at Marble head about dark; went to a Tavern, got supper, & sate talking with company till 10 & then went to bed.

[*24 March*]. Rose between 6 & 7 this morning, & notwithstanding it snowed & was extremely cold walked all over the town & examined it. Marble head is reckoned to contain more people than Salem, contains a number of fine houses, though it is extremely irregular, the Houses being built on the Top, on the sides, & at the bottom of rocks, wherever they could find a convenient situation. The harbour is very spacious, being open to the Sea at the East end, & having some Islands lying without which secures it in some measure from the Sea. I believe it is joined to the road of Salem. The Harbour is formed by a large arm of the Sea running in South west between the main & a neck of Land which lyes opposite to the town & runs Eastward till it reaches the mouth of the Harbour. It is properly a Bay or road, where the Vessels ly at anchor, & there are wharfs before the town where the Vessels come to load & unload. Before the town on the rocks are numberless Stages for drying Fish, & the same at Salem. The trade of Marble head is the same as at Salem cheifly cod, Oil & west India trade, but it is not reckoned to have so much trade as Salem. They send the best of their Fish up the Straits, & the rest to the West Indies. The best fish they catch in the winter & early in the spring, & these sometimes sells for a Guinea the Quintal, or 112 Pounds; the others in common sell for about 10 or 11 Shillings Sterling. I counted the Vessels here & there were about 60 or 70, almost all of them Schooners & sloops. The Lively man of war of 20 Guns lyes here at present.—Marble head is famous for the number of children born & brought up here. They have rope walks here as at Salem of great length.—

• • •

The Distance from M: Head to Boston is the same as from Salem to Boston, that is 20 miles. About 7 miles from Marble head the road comes into that which goes from Salem to Boston; & all this way in general the country is as bare, rocky & uncomfortable in its appearance as can well be imagined; yet the Houses are as thick seated & look as well as I ever saw in the most fertile country, which I the more observe, & so often mention as it does so much honour to the incomparable industry of the Inhabitants.

[Birket]

The Town of Portsmouth is Scituated upon Piscataway river about 3 miles from the sea upon a Moderate rising ground, not only from the river, but also from the Adjacent country to the Parade or Center thereof; where 4 Principal streets meet in the nature of a + there are pretty Streight and regular through which you have a prospect of the country on every side; the other Streets are Irregular & Crocked with many vacant lots not yet built upon, and most of em now made use of in gardens &Ca as the town Stands partly upon a point that Jetts out into the river it makes very good Conveniencys for Building wharfs and warehouses on each side out of the Strean where Ships of any Burthen may lay & discharge their cargos into the warehouses with out Expence or trouble

The houses that are of Modern Architecture are large & Exeeding neat this Sort is generally 3 Story high & well Sashed and Glazed with the best glass the rooms are well plasterd and many Wainscoted or hung with painted paper from England the outside Clapboarded very neatly and are very warm and Comodious houses one thing I observed there that they lay all there floors double, not Crossing each Other but that the seam or Joint of the uper course Shall fall upon the middle of the lower plank which prevents the air from coming thro' the floor in winter or the water falling down in Summer when they wash their houses

As to their Publick Buildings the[y] have a Church of the Established religion for church of England (which is the only one in this Government) they have also two Meeting houses for the Presbyterian or Independent perswasion All three built of wood with tall spires to each which you See a long way off at sea, indeed all the houses in town Save two are built of wood Their Court house has been formerly adwelling house and is now a Scandalous old building ready to tumble down; they have no other buildings worthy of Notice——The better sort of People here live very well and Genteel, They have no fixt market but the Country people come to town as it suits them with such of the Commoditys as they have for Sale by which the town is pretty well Supply'd with Beefe, Mutton, veal, and other Butchers Meat; they have plenty of large Hoggs and very fat bacon, they have also abundance of good fish of diferent Kinds, And abundance of Garden Culture as Beans, Peas, Carrots, Parsnips, Turnips, Radishes, Onions, Cabages Colliflowers, Asparagus, English or whats commonly called Irish Potatoes also the Sweet Potatoe,

Obtains almost alover North America, More so to southward, They have also Apples Pears, Plumbs, Cherries, & Peaches in a Abundance They have also Apricots & Nectrines from England, but do not Observe they had given any of them the Advantage of awall, there's likewise Gooseberrys Currant Ditto Rasberries, Strawberries, Huckleberries Water & Muskmellions, Squashes and Sundry Other kinds of fruits roots &c &c There common drink is Cyder which they have in great Plenty, and New England rum And also new rum from the Westindies, But People of fortune (especially the Marsh's) have very good rum and Madeira wine in their homes, Indeed the wine most commonly Drunk here is from the Canaries & Western Islands —called Oidonia, tis of a pale collor [i.e., color] tasts harsh and is inclined to look thick

There taverns are very Indifferent & little frequented by any but Strangers

This town enjoys afine Air by Standing upon arising ground and command a fine prospect from the Center every way and is Certainly the most agreeably Scituated for Pleasure or Bussiness of most places I have Seen.

12.—THE SOUTHERN PATTERNS

By mid-eighteenth century the most prominent feature of southern settlement was the independent plantation. Few were as opulent as the one described below by Philip Fithian, tutor to the Robert Carter family, but from such plantations came the elite of southern society. The more common but less dramatic pattern of settlement in the South consisted of scattered farms and small villages—the latter often no more than a cluster of houses around a store or courthouse—as a French visitor discovered in 1765.—From John Rogers Williams, ed., Philip Vickers Fithian: Journal and Letters, 1767-1774 (Princeton, 1900), pp. 128-132; and from "Journal of a French Traveler in the Colonies," American Historical Review, XXVI (1920-1921), 733-741.

[Fithian]

Mr. *Carter* now possesses 60000 Acres of Land, & about 600 Negroes—But his Estate is much divided, & lies in almost every county

in this Colony; He has Lands in the Neighbourhood of Williamsburg, & an elegant & Spacious House in that City—He owns a great
part of the well known Iron-Works near Baltimore in Maryland—
And he has one or more considerable Farms not far from Anopolis.

He has some large tracts of Land far to the West, at a place call'd
"Bull Run," & the "Great Meadows" among the mountains. He owns
land near Dumfries on the Potowmack; & large Tracts in this & the
neighbouring Counties.—Out of these Lands, which are situated so
remote from each other in various parts of these two large Provinces,
Virginia, & Maryland, Mr. Carter has chosen for the place of his
habitation a high spot of Ground in Westmoreland County at the
Head of the Navigation of the River Nomini, where he has erected
a large Elegant House, at a vast expence, which commonly goes by
the name of *Nomini-Hall*. This House is built with Brick, but the
bricks have been covered with strong lime Mortar; so that the building is now perfectly white; It is seventy-six Feet long from East to
West; & forty-four wide from North to South, two Stories high; the
Pitch of the lower story seventeen Feet, & the upper Story twelve—
It has five Stacks of Chimneys, tho' two of these serve only for ornaments.

There is a beautiful Jutt, on the South side, eighteen feet long, &
eight Feet deep from the wall which is supported by three tall pillars
—On the South side, or front, in the upper story are four Windows
each having twenty-four Lights of Glass. In the lower story are two
Windows each having forty-two Lights of Glass, & two Doors each
having Sixteen Lights—At the East end the upper story has three
Windows each with eighteen Lights; & below two Windows both
with eighteen Lights & a Door with nine—

The North side I think is the most beautiful of all; In the upper
Story is a Row of seven Windows with eighteen Lights a piece; and
below six windows, with the like number of lights; besides a large
Portico in the middle, at the sides of which are two Windows each
with eighteen Lights.—At the West end are no Windows—The
Number of Lights in all is five hundred, & forty nine—There are
four Rooms on a Floor, disposed of in the following manner. Below
is a dining Room where we usually sit; the second is a dining-Room
for the Children; the third is Mr. Carters study; & the fourth is a
Ball-Room thirty Feet long—Above stairs, one Room is for Mr.
& Mrs. Carter; the second for the ycung Ladies; & the other two
for occasional Company. As this House is large, & stands on a high
piece of Land it may be seen a considerable distance; I have seen
it at the Distance of six Miles—

At equal Distances from each corner of this Building stand four other considerable Houses, which I shall next a little describe. First, at the North East corner, & at 100 yards Distance stands the School House;

At the North-West Corner, & at the same Distance stands the stable; At the South-West Corner, & at the same Distance, stands the Coach-House; And lastly, at the South-East corner, & at an equal distance stands the Work-House. These four Houses are the corner of a Square of which the Great-House is the Center—First the School-House is forty five feet long, from East to West, & twenty-seven from North to South; It has five well-finished, convenient Rooms, three below stairs, & two above; It is built with Brick a Story and a half high with Dormant Windows; In each Room is a fire; In the large Room below-Stairs we keep our School; the other two Rooms below which are smaller are allowed to Mr. Randolph the Clerk; The Room above the School-Room Ben and I live in; & the other Room above Stairs belongs to *Harry* & *Bob*. Five of us live in this House with great Neatness, & convenience; each one has a Bed to himself—

And we are call'd by the Bell to the Great-House to Breakfast &c—The Wash-House is built in the same form, & is of the same Size of the School-House—From the front yard of the Great House, to the Wash-House is a curious *Terrace,* covered finely with Green turf, & about five foot high with a slope of eight feet, which appears exceeding well to persons coming to the front of the House—This *Terrace* is produced along the Front of the House, and ends by the Kitchen; but before the Front-Doors is a broad flight of steps of the same Height, & slope of the *Terrace.*

The Stable & coach-House are of the same Length & Breadth as the School-and Wash-House, only they are higher pitched to be convenient for holding Hay & Fodder.

Due East of the Great House are two Rows of tall, flourishing, beautiful, Poplars, beginning on a Line drawn from the School to the Wash-House; these Rows are something wider than the House, & are about 300 yards Long, at the Eastermost end of which is the great Road leading through Westmoreland to Richmond. These Rows of Poplars form an extremely pleasant avenue, & at the Road, through them, the House appears most romantic, at the same time that it does truly elegant—The Area of the Triangle made by the Wash-House, Stable, & School-House is perfectly livel, & designed for a bowling-Green, laid out in rectangular Walks which are paved with Brick, & covered over with burnt Oyster-Shells—In the other Tri-

angle, made by the Wash-House, Stable, & Coach-House is the
Kitchen, a well-built House, as large as the School-House; Bake-
House; Dairy; Store-House & several other small Houses; all which
stand due West, & at a small distance from the great House, & form
a little handsome Street. These Buildings stand about a quarter of
a Mile from a Fork of the River Nomini, one Branch of which runs
on the East of us, on which are two Mills; one of them belongs to
Mr. Turburville the other to Mr. Washington, both within a mile—
another branch of the River runs on the West of us, on which and
at a small distance above the House stands Mr. Carters Merchant
Mill . . . ; to go to the mill from the House we descend I imagine
about an 100 Feet; the Dam is so broad that two carriages may pass
conveniently on it; & the Pond from twelve to Eighteen Foot water
—at the fork Mr. Carter has a Granary, where he lands his Wheat
for the mill, Iron from the Works &c—

∽

[French Traveler]

fryday 15th [1765]. Set out from the vessel with my servant and
portmantle on his Sholder. we walked 7 miles to where there were
some whale fishers tents, and got one of them to Cary us over the
Sound in their boat to Beaufort, a Small vilage not above 12 houses,
the inhabitants seem miserable, they are very lasy and Indolent, they
live mostly on fish and oisters, which they have here in great plenty.
this harbour is Calld topsail inlet or Cor sound. Non but small vessels
Can come here there being but 13 feet water on the bar at low water.
the tide does not rise above 4 feet. . . . the litle trade that is Caryed
on here Consists in terpentine, tar and pitch. . . .

Saturday March the 16th. 1765. got horsses with great Difficulty
for myself, servant and a guide, and rode through a Continual forest
of pine trees, with narrow roads Cut in Diferent points of the Compas
(it would be necessary to have one to travel in this Country) until we
Came to a good Quakers 12 miles Dist. from Beaufort, where I lay
this night. he makes spirits of terpentine and rosin.

Sunday 17th Do. Departed from the quakers Early in the morning
for new Burn [Newbern] and still the same thing today as yesterday,
pine trees, In general terpentine walks, there is also oak and sipres
and some sedr; there was here and there a small vilage and some litle
farms Dispersd up and Down where they rais nothing but Indian
Corn (of which they make their bread) and peas. the Soil all along

very sandy and indifferent, the land Extremly level and Even, not the least apearance of a Small hill, nor a stone to be Seen, but sea shels in plenty, which would seem to intimate that great part of Carolina was risen by the sands thrown up by the Sea to a Certain hight and then obliged itself to retire. the roads here must be very Dangerous in stormy weather by the falling of great Dead trees. the Inhabitants are obliged by an act of assembly to Cut them when once Dead but they are not very punctual in the Execution therof. at 5 arived at trent river fery, a Small mile over to Newburn, which is to be the Capitol of north Carolina, as being best situated for that purpose; it is the most sentrical town in the province, on a point that seperates the two rivers. . . . there is plenty of saw mills in this Country set up at litle Expence. wherever there is water that they can raise to the hight of 5 feet by means of a Dam or breastworks they Erect a mill, if there is a sufficient quantity of water; the wheels are undershot about 3½ foot Diameter and 10 or 12 in length, they are allways going, as the Contry is Cover with timber such as pitch pine, read, black, and white oak (the two first are very bad wood), some walnut, sipres and sedar, they are always well suplied. there is generaly a tub mil for grinding their Corn at the same Dam. In the spring of the year, there is great quantitys of herin Catched in the Diferent rivers, also shad (which we Call allose in france), Drum and sturgeon; they send this fish to the westindia Islands, and the parts of the Continent where is non Catched; there grows some wheat in this province, but in small quantity, the Soil not Suiting it. their bread is generally of Indian meal. the town Consists of about 100 houses and 500 Inhabitants. there is a good Church and Courthouse. this place is very unhealthy in the sumertime, as is all Carolina, much aflicted with feavors, which must be owing to the lands being very low and not Cleard of the wood, and the stagnateing waters of these great rivers where there is no tide or Curent but what is occasioned by the winds. on hot Calm Days youl see a thick scum on the water, which occasions a Disagreable stensh. at this time the fishes ly Dead on the water.

• • •

Saturday march the 23d 1765. Set out from Newburn (where I eat my St. Patricks Dinner which lasted untill 4 next morning), took fery a mile from the town and Crossed News river, which is about 2 miles broad here, but full of shoals. saw several flats Coming Down with pitch and tar, Corn, shingles, etc. Came this night to Mrs. bonds fery oposit to bath town,

Do 24th. Crossd over to bath. the fery is three miles Including one mile up the Creek on which the town lies. bath is small having but litle or no trade. . . .

        •   •   •

wednesday march the 27th 1765. Set out from bath, Crossed through forests and uncultivated lands as before to this Difference, the Soil seems to beter gradualy as I Come to the norwd., and a greater mixture of oak trees than hitherto . . . Great troops or flocks of swine which run wild in the woods and feed on the pine seeds and acorns, which is their only food. it is not surprising that their pork is not so firm or good in any sheap [shape] as to the norwd. where they feed them with Corn etc. there is great plenty of Dear in this part of Country, but will soon Diminish, if they Continue Destroying as they do now, in season or out of season, male or female is all alike. . . . it is Computed that 6000 hhds. of tobaco are sent from this part, to Petersbourg on James's river, virginia. there Comes a Considerable quantity of wheat and Corn Down this river, and about 3000 hhds. tobaco which is shiped at Edenton. the Soil along the Sides of this river is rekoned fertil and rich, which is owing to its yearly overflow, it has that in Common with the nile In Egipt. but it a Dangerous neighbour when in that state, for it sometimes rises 40 feet perpindicular and Carys Every thing on its way, before it. it Covers great part of the adjacint Country as it is so very flat and level. the floods or freshes are generaly in the End of septe'r and begining of octob'r. there are plenty of Iron mines in this part of the province but not yet worked; . . .

        •   •   •

by Computation, there is in this province from 25 to 30 thousand white taxables, or men from the age of 16 to 60—whom are musterd 4 times a year as militia; there but very few if any rich people. their fortunes Consist generally in lands, which are for the most part uncultivated, and Consequently of no advantage or value for the present, but the Inhabitants augment fast. this province is the azilum of the Convicts that have served their time in virginia and maryland. when at liberty they all (or great part) Come to this part where they are not Known and setle here. it is a fine Country for poor people, but not for the rich.

        •   •   •

aipril the 17th. Set out for portsmouth which is 30 miles. Dined at Robertses ordinary. arived at portsmouth at 6 in the Evening. the Country along something more open and Inhabited, but still very thick in wood. about 7 miles from Robertses Crossed the End of the Dismal swamp. this is a Considerable tract of land buried under water.

there is a lake in the midle. this swamp is a harbour for all sorts of willd beasts, such as Bears, panters, woolfs, and great quantity of serpents.

Portsmouth is situated on the west Side of Elizabeth river, oposite to Norfolk, which is on the East side and Capitale of a County of its name. Portsmouth is but lately setled. it has the advantage of norfolk haveing Deeper water of its side. ships of any Burden Can Come Close [to] the wharfs of which there are several very Convenient. norfolk on the other hand has been longer setled. it is the most Considerable town for trade and shiping In virginia. this harbour is very safe for ships of any Burthen. this is the only part of virginia where they build any thing of ships. the[y] have all the Conveniencies imaginable for that purpose. there is a fine ropery here, there are plenty of masts of all proportions to be had, and great quantitys are shiped of for all parts, Especially for the havana where they have a Contract for this article. there is a Smart trade Caried on from Norfolk to the wes[t] India Islands. their exports Consists in pork, Corn, flower, Butter, Cheese, Candles. hogs fat, tallow, ham, Bacon, lumber of all kinds, shingles, Masts, Yards, and naval stores; hemp is very much encouraged now, in virginia. and grows to great perfection. Iron they have great plenty of, it is brought Down here from maryland, and sold at the rate of 10 ps. p. tun. . . .

•   •   •

aipril the 24th. Set out for williamsburg In Company with andrew sprowl Esqr. and several of the Norfolk Gentlemen. left my horses at the tavern where I lodge; we took boat and Crossed over to hampton where we Dined. this fery is 12 miles across. hampton is a small town of very little trade, but the Navall and Colectors offices being here makes it more Considerable than it otherwise would be. it has no harbour. there is a bar Crosses it about 2 miles Dist. from the town, outside of which, ships that are bound up or Down Jameses river (on the North side of which this town is placed) Come to an anchor and take their Expeditions. small Craft Can go over this Bar and ly Close to the town.

from hampton to york 28 miles. here we lay. this is a fine situation and a very prety litle town Inhabited by some of the genteelest people In virginia, who have some very prety buildings here. it is on an Elevated spot of grownd by the side of the river to which it gives its name, on which it has a beautiful prospect. ships of any burthen Can Come here, and 40 miles farther up. there was at this time three large vessels rideing of here. this and hampton road are the general rendevous for the homeward bound ships. in war time there are on such occasions 100 sail of shiping to be seen here. the Country about here is very agreable. there is a small town on the oposite side of the river Called Gloster, of no great note. its situation is also very pleasant. there was a great Deal of Company at our tavern this night, several Capns. of ships, looking for freight, others gathering their funds.

aipril the 25th. set out Early for williamsburg, 12 miles Distn. fine road and pleasant Country. at 9 arived at this Capitol, which at a Distance looks like a large town, but it is far from it and very Iregular haveing only one street which Can be Called so, which makes a very good apearance. it is very s[p]acious, has at one End the Capitolle, a very good building in the form of an Each. the Court is held in one wing on the first floor, the assembly room is in the other wing on the Same floor, the Councill and Comitee Chambers are upstairs on the first story. oposite to this building at the further End of the street Is a very fine Colege, which makes a grand apearance. halfway betwixt these Builds. is the Church on one side the street and the powder magazeen on the other. the Governors house is towards the Colege on its left a litle back from the main street. it is a Small but neat building, with a Cupula on the top.

13.—URBAN AMERICA

By the eve of the Revolution, several major cities had grown out of the American wilderness. Boston, New York, Charleston, and Newport were thriving centers of population and trade, while Philadelphia had become the second largest city in the British Empire. An impression of New York—which during the half-century before the Revolution supplanted Boston as second city in British America—was recorded by Patrick M'Robert in the summer of 1774.— From Carl Bridenbaugh, ed., "Patrick M'Robert's Tour Through Part of the North Provinces of America," The Pennsylvania Magazine of History and Biography, *LIX (1935), 138-142.*

. . . New Jersey and Staten Island on the west, and Long Island on the east [form] the mouth of Hudson's river, and harbour of New York. On both sides of the harbour, the woods, country houses, orchards, and fields of Indian corn, form at this season of the year a beautiful prospect. There is very good water up to New York, the harbour is spacious and large, with many convenient docks or quays, with store-houses upon them for vessels of any burden to lie always afloat along side of them. Here are at present upward of 300 sail of shipping. They carry on an extensive trade from this port to Britain, Ireland, Holland, France, Spain, Portugal, up the Mediterranian, the West Indies, Spanish Main, as well as to the other colonies. Their exports are chiefly wheat, flour, Indian corn, indigo, flaxseed, pot and pearl ashes, fish, oil, pork, iron, timber, lumber, wax, and live cattle to the West Indies. Their imports are from Britain all kinds of cloth, linen and woolen, wrought iron, shoes, stockings, &c. From Holland, they have Europian and East India goods; from France, Spain and Portugal, wines, spirits, fruits, silks, and other articles of luxury; from the Spanish Main, they have log-wood, mahogany, some indigo and dollars; from the West Indies, they have sugar, rum and molasses. Another considerable article of their export is built vessels, a good many of which are now on the stocks at this port, which they generally load with their own produce, and carry to some market where they sell both ship and cargo. They have great choice of wood in their ship-yards. Their upper timbers they make all of cedar, which they prefer to oak. They are very nice in the workmanship of ship-building here, and use a great deal of ornament and painting about the vessels.

•   •   •

New York is situate about 41 degrees north latitude and 74 degrees west longitude from London, upon the south end of an island, of about fourteen or fifteen miles in length, and between two and three broad, formed by a branch of Hudson's river running into the east river, or Sound that divides Long Island from the continent. The situation is extremely pleasant, upon a rising ground from the shore or river on both sides. The city is large, and contains a great many neat buildings. The publick buildings, and places of worship, are generally very neat, and well finished, if not elegant. The college, tho' only one third of the plan is compleat, makes a fine appearance, on one of the finest situations perhaps of any college in the world. Here are taught divinity, mathematicks, the practice and theory of medicine, chymistry, surgery, and materia medica. One circumstance I think is a little unlucky, the enterance to this college is thro' one of the streets where the most noted prostitutes live. This is certainly a temptation to the youth that have occasion to pass so often that way.

The new hospital tho' not quite finished is another fine building upon the same plan as the Royal Infirmary at Edinburgh. The goal [gaol?] makes a fine appearance without, and if as agreeable within, I do not wonder to hear of its being pretty full. The city hall, the exchange, the workhouse, are all neat brick buildings. Here are also neat barracks for about 500 men. They have three English churchs, three Presbyterian, two Dutch Lutheran, two Dutch Calvenists, all neat and well finished buildings, besides a French church, an Anabaptist, a Methodist, a Quaker meeting, a Moravian church, and a Jews synagogue. There are many other fine buildings belonging to private gentlemen and merchants; but the streets are in general ill paved, irregular, and too narrow. There are four market places, as well supplied with all kinds of provisions.

They are pretty well supplied with fresh water from pumps sunk at convenient distances in the streets. Their tea water they get at present brought in carts thro' the streets from the suburbs of the city; but they are now erecting a fire engine for raising the spring into a reservoir, from whence, by pipes, they can convey it to any part of the city. They are pretty well guarded against accidents from fire, by obliging every citizen to register their house, and for one shilling a vent yearly, to have them swept once a month They have also a number of engines kept at convenient distances: to each of these is appointed a captain, and a certain number of men. And when a fire happens, a premium is always allowed to the captain and his men who can first make their engines play upon the fire. By this precaution fire seldom happens, and by the proper disposition of the engines, when it does happen, it is seldom allowed to spread farther than the house it brakes out in.

The streets are agreeably shaded in some parts with trees. They have a fort, but of no great strength, and a battery with a good number of guns mounted, which may command that part of the harbour between New York and the Governor's Island. Near the fort is an equestrian statue of king George the III. upon an elegant pedestial in the middle of a fine green rail'd in with iron. At the crossing of two public streets, stands at full length a marble statute of lord Chatham erected by the citizens in gratitude for his strenuous opposition to the stamp act in 1766 They have several large roperies, distilleries, breweries, and a large iron work carried on here. They have plenty of mechanicks of all kinds, by whom almost every thing that is made with you in Britain is made to as great perfection here. The inhabitants are in general brisk and lively, kind to strangers, dress very gay; the fair sex are in general handsome, and said to be very obliging. Above 500 ladies of pleasure keep lodgings contiguous within the consecreated liberties of St. Paul's. This part of the city belongs to the church, and has thence obtained the name of the *Holy Ground*. Here all the prostitutes reside, among whom are many fine well dressed women, and it is remarkable that they live in much greater cordiality one with another than any nests of that kind do in Britain or Ireland.

It rather hurts an Europian eye to see so many negro slaves upon the streets, tho' they are said to deminish yearly here. The city is governed by a mayor, and divided into seven different wards, over each of which an alderman and an assistant presides. They have generally the same laws and regulations as is in England. There are computed between twenty-six and thirty thousand inhabitants in the city; in this number are, I believe, included the slaves, who make at least a fifth part of the number.

14.—FRONTIER LIFE

To some observers the back-country settlements seemed a refuge for criminals and reprobates; to others American life there was most pure and free. Both viewpoints are reflected in the following impressions—the first a generally favorable account by Joseph Doddridge who was raised on the western frontier of Pennsylvania and Virginia; the second a mixed reaction by an English-bred Anglican clergyman from Charleston, South Carolina, who served during the 1760s as a missionary to the Carolina frontiersmen.— From Joseph Doddridge, Notes on the Settlement and Indian Wars . . . *(Pittsburgh, 1912), pp. 80-84, 88-89, 91-93; and from Charles Woodmason,* The Carolina Backcountry on the Eve of the Revolution, *ed. Richard J. Hooker (Chapel Hill, 1953), pp. 77-78, 80-81.*

[Doddridge]

The settlements on this side of the mountains commenced along the Monongahela, and between that river and the Laurel Ridge, in the year 1772. In the succeeding year they reached the Ohio river. The greater number of the first settlers came from the upper parts of . . . Maryland and Virginia. Braddock's trail, as it was called, was the route by which the greater number of them crossed the mountains. A less number of them came by the way of Bedford and Fort Ligonier, the military road from Pennsylvania to Pittsburg. They effected their removals on horses furnished with pack-saddles. This was the more easily done, as but few of these early adventurers into the wilderness were encumbered with much baggage.

•   •   •

There was, at an early period of our settlements, an inferior kind of land title denominated a *tomahawk right,* which was made by deadening a few trees near the head of a spring, and marking the bark of some one or more of them with the initials of the name of the person who made the improvement. I remember having seen a number of these tomahawk rights when a boy. For a long time many of them bore the names of those who made them. I have no knowledge of the efficacy of the tomahawk improvement, or whether it conferred any right whatever, unless followed by an actual settlement. These rights, however, were often bought and sold. Those who wished to make settlement on their favorite tracts of land bought up the tomahawk improvements rather than enter into quarrels with those who had made them. Other improvers of the land, with a view to actual settlement, and who happened to be stout veteran fellows, took a very different course from that of purchasing the tomahawk rights. When annoyed by the claimants under those rights they deliberately cut a few good hickories and gave them what was called in those days *a laced jacket,* that is a sound whipping.

Some of the early settlers took the precaution to come over the mountains in the spring, leaving their families behind to raise a crop of corn, and then return and bring them out in the fall. This I should think was the better way. Others, especially those whose families were small, brought them with them in the spring. My father took the latter course. His family was but small and he brought them all with him. The Indian meal which he brought over the mountain was expended six weeks too soon, so that for that length of time we had to live without bread. The lean venison and the breast of the wild turkey we were taught to call bread. The flesh of the bear was denominated meat. This artifice did not succeed very well; after living in this way for some time we became sickly, the stomach seemed to be always empty, and tormented with a sense of hunger. I remember how narrowly the children watched the growth of the potato tops, pumpkin and squash vines, hoping from day to day to get something to answer in the place of bread. How delicious was the taste of the young potatoes when we got them! What a jubilee when we were permitted to pull the young corn for roasting ears! Still more so when it had acquired sufficient hardness to be made into johnny cakes by the aid of a tin grater. We then became healthy, vigorous and contented with our situation, poor as it was.

My father with a small number of his neighbors made their settlements in the spring of 1773. Though they were in a poor and destitute situation, they nevertheless lived in peace; but their tranquility was not of long continuance. Those most atrocious murders of the peaceable inoffensive Indians at Captina and Yellow Creek brought on the war of Lord Dunmore in the spring of the year 1774. Our little settlement then broke up. The women and children were removed to Morris' fort in Sandy creek glade, some distance to the east of Uniontown. The fort consisted of an assemblage of small hovels, situated on the margin of a large and noxious marsh, the effluvia of which gave the most of the women and children the fever and ague. The men were compelled by necessity to return home, and risk the tomahawk and scalping knife of the Indians, in raising corn to keep their families from starvation the succeeding winter. Those sufferings, dangers and losses, were the tribute we had to pay to that thirst for blood which actuated those veteran murderers who brought the war upon us! . . .

•   •   •

My father, like many others, believed, that having secured his legal allotment, the rest of the country belonged of right to those who chose to settle in it. There was a piece of vacant land adjoining his tract amounting to about two hundred acres. To this tract of land he had the preemption right, and accordingly secured it by warrant; but his conscience would not permit him to retain it in his family; he therefore gave it to an apprentice lad whom he had raised in his house. This lad sold it to an uncle of mine for a cow and a calf and a wool hat.

•   •   •

The furniture for the table, for several years after the settlement of this country, consisted of a few pewter dishes, plates and spoons; but mostly of wooden bowls, trenchers and noggins. If these last were scarce, gourds and hard shelled squashes made up the deficiency. The iron pots, knives and forks, were brought from the east side of the mountains along with the salt and iron on pack horses. These articles of furniture corresponded very well with the articles of diet on which they were employed. "Hog and hominy" were proverbial for the dish of which they were the component parts. Johnny cake and pone were at the outset of the settlements of the country the only forms of bread in use for breakfast and dinner. At supper, milk and mush was the standard dish. When milk was not plenty, which was often the case, owing to the scarcity of cattle, or the want of proper pasture for them, the substantial dish of hominy had to supply the place of them; mush was frequently eaten with sweetened water, molasses, bear's oil, or the gravy of fried meat.

Every family, besides a little garden for the few vegetables which they cultivated, had another small enclosure containing from half an acre to an acre, which they called a *truck patch,* in which they raised corn for roasting ears, pumpkins, squashes, beans and potatoes. These, in the latter part of the summer and fall, were cooked with their pork, venison and bear meat for dinner, and made very wholesome and well tasted dishes. The standard dinner dish for every log rolling, house raising and harvest day was a pot pie, or what in other countries is called *sea pie.* This, besides answering for dinner, served for a part of the supper also. The remainder of it from dinner, being eaten with milk in the evening, after the conclusion of the labor of the day.

In our whole display of furniture, the delft, china and silver were unknown. It did not then as now require contributions from the four quarters of the globe to furnish the breakfast table, viz: the silver from Mexico; the coffee from the West Indies; the tea from China, and the delft and porcelain from Europe or Asia. Yet our homely fare, and unsightly cabins, and furniture, produced a hardy veteran race, who planted the first footsteps of society and civilization in the immense regions of the west. Inured to hardihood, bravery and labor from their early youth, they sustained with manly fortitude the fatigue of the chase, the campaign and scout, and with strong arms "turned the wilderness into fruitful fields." . . .

• • •

On the frontiers, and particularly amongst those who were much in the habit of hunting, and going on scouts and campaigns, the dress of the men was partly Indian and partly that of civilized nations.

The hunting shirt was universally worn. This was a kind of loose frock, reaching half way down the thighs, with large sleeves, open before, and so wide as to lap over a foot or more when belted. The cap was large, and sometimes handsomely fringed with a ravelled piece of cloth of a different color from that of the hunting shirt itself. The bosom of this dress served as a wallet to hold a chunk of bread, cakes, jerk, tow for wiping the barrel of the rifle, or any other necessary for the hunter or warrior. The belt, which was always tied behind, answered several purposes, besides that of holding the dress together. In cold weather the mittens, and sometimes the bullet-bag, occupied the front part of it. To the right side was suspended the tomahawk and to the left the scalping knife in its leathern sheath. The hunting shirt was generally made of linsey, sometimes of coarse linen, and a few of dressed deer skins. These last were very cold and uncomfortable in wet weather. The shirt and jacket were of the common fashion. A pair of drawers or breeches and leggins were the dress of the thigh and legs; a pair of moccasins answered for the feet much better than shoes. These were made of dressed deer skin. They were mostly made of a single piece with a gathering seam along the top of the foot, and another from the bottom of the heel, without gathers as high as the ankle joint or a little higher. Flaps were left on each side to reach some distance up the legs. These were nicely adapted to the ankles and lower part of the leg by thongs of deer skin, so that no dust, gravel or snow could get within the moccasin.

The moccasins in ordinary use cost but a few hours labor to make them. This was done by an instrument denominated a moccasin awl, which was made of the backspring of an old claspknife. This awl with its buckshorn handle was an appendage of every shot pouch strap, together with a roll of buckskin for mending the moccasins. This was the labor of almost every evening. They were sewed together and patched with deer skin thongs, or whangs, as they were commonly called.

In cold weather the moccasins were well stuffed with deer's hair, or dry leaves, so as to keep the feet comfortably warm; but in wet weather it was usually said that wearing them was "a decent way of going barefooted;" and such was the fact, owing to the spongy texture of the leather of which they were made.

Owing to this defective covering of the feet, more than to any other circumstance, the greater number of our hunters and warriors were afflicted with the rheumatism in their limbs. Of this disease they were all apprehensive in cold or wet weather, and therefore always slept with their feet to the fire to prevent or cure it as well as they could. This practice unquestionably had a very salutary effect, and prevented many of them from becoming confirmed cripples in early life.

In the latter years of the Indian war our young men became more enamored of the Indian dress throughout, with the exception of the matchcoat. The drawers were laid aside and the leggins made longer, so as to reach the upper part of the thigh. The Indian breech clout was adopted. This was a piece of linen or cloth nearly a yard long, and eight or nine inches broad. This passed under the belt before and behind leaving the ends for flaps hanging before and behind over the belt. These flaps were sometimes ornamented with some coarse kind of embroidery work. To the same belts which secured the breech clout, strings which supported the long leggins were attached. When this belt, as was often the case, passed over the hunting shirt the upper part of the thighs and part of the hips were naked.

The young warrior instead of being abashed by this nudity was proud of his Indian like dress. In some few instances I have seen them go into places of public worship in this dress. Their appearance, however, did not add much to the devotion of the young ladies.

The linsey petticoat and bed gown, which were the universal dress of our women in early times, would make a strange figure in our days. . . .

They went barefooted in warm weather, and in cold their feet were covered with moccasins, coarse shoes, or shoepacks. . . .

The coats and bedgowns of the women, as well as the hunting shirts of the men, were hung in full display on wooden pegs round the walls of their cabins, so that while they answered in some degree the place of paper hangings or tapestry they announced to the stranger as well as neighbor the wealth or poverty of the family in the articles of clothing. . . .

~~

[Woodmason]

In the Back Part of this Country between the Heads of Pedee and Cape Fear Rivers, is a Distric[t] of 12,000 Acres, formerly granted to Whitfield, and by Him sold to Count Zinzendorff—It is very rich Land—scituated just at foot of the lower Hills, and where the Springs take their Rise, that form these Great Rivers above mentioned. The Spot is not only Rich, fertile, and luxuriant, but the most Romantic in Nature. Sir Philip Sidneys Description of Arcadia, falls short of this *real* Arcadia. . . . To this Spot Zinzindorff transplanted his Hernhutters; who being join'd by others from Pensylvania, and Elsewhere now form a very large and numerous Body of People, Acting under their own Laws and Ordinances, independent of the Community, Constitution or Legislature in and over them. They are a Set of *Recabites* among the People of *Israel*—Forming a Distinc[t] Body, different in all things from All People. Here they have laid out two Towns—*Bethelem* and *Bethsada;* delightfully charming! Rocks, Cascades, Hills, Vales, Groves, Plains—Woods, Waters all most strangely intermixt, so that Imagination cannot paint any thing more vivid They have Mills, Furnaces, Forges, Potteries,

Founderies All Trades, and all things in and among themselves—
Their Manners are not unlike the *Dunkers* of *Pensylvania:* Like them,
they have All things (save Women) in Common; and receive to
their Community Persons of all Nations, Religion and Language.
They are seated near some valuable Copper Mines, from which they
draw Great Advantage; And having all things free, setting all Hands
at Work according to their Ability (for they are all *Bees,* not a Drone
suffer'd in the Hive) What they do not consume they sell in the
Adjacent Territory, Receiving for their Meal, Flour, Earthen Ware,
Peach-Brandy, Whisky—Tools of Iron and Utensils of Copper, Wood
and Turnery Wares &c. &c. Deer Skins, Fox, Otter, Raccoon, and
other Furs and Peltry—These they send off into Virginia on the
one Hand, and into South Carolina on the other—Receiving in Return Rum, Sugar, Linen and Woollen Goods—Pewter and Tin Wares,
and other Necessaries.

•   •   •

The Manners of the North Carolinians in General, are Vile and
Corrupt—The whole Country is a Stage of Debauchery Dissoluteness
and Corruption—And how can it be otherwise? The People are
compos'd of the Out Casts of all the other Colonies who take Refuge
there. The Civil Police is hardly yet establish'd. But they are so
numerous—The Necessaries of Life are so cheap, and so easily acquir'd, and propagation being unrestricted, that the Encrease of
People there, is inconceivable, even to themselves.

Marriages (thro' want of Clergy) are perform'd by ev'ry ordinary
Magistrate. Polygamy is very Common—Celibacy much more—Bas-
tardy, no disrepute—Concubinage General—When will this *Augean*
Stable be cleans'd!

IV

Zeal
for Education

Regardless of where and how a settler chose to live, an important part of his happiness depended on the degree to which he took advantage of Colonial America's opportunities. Success was not merely for the asking. Energy, perseverance, family connections, and luck all helped to determine the limits of achievement in the New World. But increasingly Americans came to believe that knowledge, above anything else, held the key to personal and public advancement. By the middle of the eighteenth century, Americans exhibited an almost universal zeal for education.

Colonists who stopped to consider their educational institutions were confronted by a confusing variety of sizes, qualities, and purposes. Prior to the start of his formal schooling the colonial youth learned the rudiments of the three Rs from his parents, or perhaps from a tutor, or in a local parsonage, or at a town school. He then went on to a grammar school where the intricacies of language and related subjects were imparted to budding scholars. But even these institutions followed no set pattern: some were public, some private, some a curious combination; some stressed classical languages, others emphasized English, still others specialized in "practical subjects."

For boys willing and able to study beyond the grammar school, Colonial America offered several choices. Of the colonial colleges Harvard was, of course, the oldest and most distinguished, but before the Revolution put a temporary end to formal learning, eight other colleges had emerged to break the Massachusetts monopoly on higher education. If the colonial colleges were small, denominational (except

73

Benjamin Franklin's College of Philadelphia), and unsophisticated by European standards, they at least reflected the provincial American's determination to educate himself.

Equally revealing is the proliferation of private schools and special courses that appeared in the eighteenth century to supplement the more formal institutions. Judging from the frequency of newspaper advertisements for dancing schools, reading schools, navigation schools, fencing lessons, and shorthand lessons, Colonial Americans were eager for learning of almost any kind.

At the same time, other institutions, not strictly academic, contributed importantly to American education. For thousands upon thousands of colonial youths, apprenticeship to a master craftsman served as vocational training; so too did indentured servitude for young men and women who came to America without highly developed skills. And even where educational institutions were at their best, the family and the church performed major roles in the training of youth. The head of a household had a legal as well as a moral obligation to provide his wards with learning, and in rural areas the family often imparted to its members much of the academic and all of the vocational training they ever received. Similarly the church—regardless of denomination—accepted responsibility for the moral, spiritual, and social indoctrination of its young people; most churches also actively encouraged scholastic achievement. From the perspective of the twentieth century it is clear that education in pre-Revolutionary America made up in enthusiasm and diversity much of what it lacked in formality.

15.—COLONIAL SCHOOLDAYS

In most New England towns and in cities throughout British America, boys attended public or private writing schools from about six to eight years of age. Some went no further, but those who wanted additional training for its own sake or who aspired to a college education enrolled in an academy or Latin grammar school until the age of about fifteen. Alexander Graydon, who spent most of his boyhood in Philadelphia, wrote the following recollections.—From Memoirs of a Life of Alexander Graydon . . . (*Harrisburgh, 1811*), *pp. 13-17, 24-26, 30 31.*

There being no traces in my memory, of any incidents worthy of remark, during the period of my infancy, I pass on to the era of my removal to Philadelphia, for the sake of my education. This, I suppose to have been, between my sixth and seventh year. . . . In the city, I lived with, and was under the care of my grandfather. The school he first put me to, was that of David James Dove, an Englishman, and much celebrated in his day, as a teacher, and no less as a dealer in the minor kind of satirical poetry. . . . It was his practice in his school, to substitute disgrace for corporal punishment. His birch was rarely used in canonical method, but was generally stuck into the back part of the collar of the unfortunate culprit, who, with this badge of disgrace towering from his nape like a broom at the mast-head of a vessel for sale, was compelled to take his stand upon the top of the form, for such a period of time, as his offence was thought to deserve. He had another contrivance for boys who were late in their morning attendance. This was to dispatch a committee of five or six scholars for them, with a bell and lighted lantern, and in this "odd equipage," in broad day light, the bell all the while dingling, were they escorted through the streets to school. As Dove affected a strict regard to justice in his dispensations of punishment, and always professed a willingness, to have an equal measure of it meted out to himself in case of his transgressing, the boys took him at his word; and one morning, when he had overstaid his time, either through laziness, inattention or design, he found himself waited on in the usual form. He immediately admitted the justice of the procedure, and putting himself behind the lantern and bell, marched with great solemnity to school, to the no small gratification of the boys, and entertainment of the spectators. But this incident took place before I became a scholar. It was once my lot to be attended in this manner, but what had been sport to my tutor, was to me a serious punishment.

The school was at this time, kept in Videll's alley, which opened into Second, a little below Chesnut street. It counted a number of scholars of both sexes, though chiefly boys; and the assistant or writing master, was John Reily, a very expert penman and conveyancer, a man of some note, who, in his gayer moods affected a pompous and technical phraseology. . . . I know not what my progress was under the auspices of Mr. Dove, but having never in my early years, been smitten with the love of learning, I have reason to conclude, it did not pass mediocrity. . . .

Being now, probably, about eight years of age, it was deemed expedient to enter me at the academy, then, as it now continues to be, under the name of a university, the principal seminary in Pennsylvania; and I was accordingly introduced by my father, to Mr. Kinnesley, the teacher of English and professor of oratory. He was an Anabaptist clergyman, a large, venerable looking man, of no great general erudition, though a considerable proficient in electricity; and who, whether truly or not, has been said to have had a share in certain discoveries in that science, of which doctor Franklin received the whole credit. The task, of the younger boys, at least, consisted in learning to read and to write their mother tongue grammatically; and one day in the week (I think Friday) was set apart for the recitation of select passages in poetry and prose. For this purpose, each scholar, in his turn, ascended the stage, and said his speech, as the phrase was. This speech was carefully taught him by his master, both with respect to its pronunciation, and the action deemed suitable to its several parts. Two of these specimens of infantile oratory, to the disturbance of my repose, I had been qualified to exhibit: Family partiality, no doubt, overrated their merit; and hence, my declaiming powers were in a state of such constant requisition, that my orations, like worn out ditties, became vapid and fatiguing to me; and consequently, impaired my relish for that kind of acquirement. More profit attended my reading. After Aesop's fables, and an abridgment of the Roman history, Telemachus was put into our hands; and if it be admitted that the human heart may be bettered by instruction, mine, I may aver, was benefitted by this work of the virtuous Fenelon. While the mild wisdom of Mentor called forth my veneration, the noble ardor of the youthful hero excited my sympathy and emulation. I took part, like a second friend, in the vicissitudes of his fortune, I participated in his toils, I warmed with his exploits, I wept where he wept, and exulted where he triumphed. . . .

•   •   •

[In the spring of 1761] I was about to enter the Latin school. The person whose pupil I was consequently to become, was Mr. John Beveridge, a native of Scotland, who retained the smack of his vernacular tongue in its primitive purity. His acquaintance with the language he taught, was I believe, justly deemed to be very accurate and profound. But as to his other acquirements, after excepting the game of backgammon, in which he was said to excel, truth will not warrant me in saying a great deal. He was, however, diligent and laborious in his attention to his school; and had he possessed the faculty of making himself beloved by the scholars, and of exciting their emulation and exertion, nothing would have been wanting in him to an entire qualification for his office. But unfortunately, he had no dignity of character, and was no less destitute of the art of making himself respected than beloved. Though not perhaps to be complained of as intolerably severe, he yet made a pretty free use of the ratan and the ferule [switches for disciplining students], but to very little purpose. He was in short no disciplinarian, and consequently, very unequal to the management of seventy or eighty boys, many of whom were superlatively pickle and unruly. He was assisted, indeed, by two ushers, who eased him in the burden of teaching, but who, in matters of discipline, seemed disinclined to interfere, and disposed to consider themselves rather as subjects than rulers. I have seen them slyly slip out of the way when the principal was entering upon the job of capitally punishing a boy, who from his size, would be likely to make resistance. For this had become nearly a matter of course; and poor Beveridge, who was diminutive in his stature and neither young nor vigorous, after exhausting himself in the vain attempt to denude the delinquent, was generally glad to compound, for a few strokes over his clothes, on any part that was accessible. He had, indeed, so frequently been foiled, that his birch at length was rarely brought forth, and might truly be said to have lose its terrors. . . . He indemnified himself, however, by a redoubled use of his ratan.

So entire was the want of respect towards him, and so liable was he to be imposed upon, that one of the larger boys, for a wager, once pulled off his wig, which he effected by suddenly twitching it from his head under pretence of brushing from it a spider; and the unequivocal insult was only resented by the peevish exclamation of *hoot mon!*

Various were the rogueries that were played upon him; but the most audacious of all was the following. At the hour of convening in the afternoon, that being found the most convenient, from the circumstance of Mr. Beveridge being usually a little beyond the time; the bell having rung, the ushers being at their posts, and the scholars arranged in their classes, three or four of the conspirators conceal themselves without, for the purpose of observing the motions of their victim. He arrives, enters the school, and is permitted to proceed until he is supposed to have nearly reached his chair at the upper end of the room, when instantly the door and every window-shutter is closed. Now, shrouded in utter darkness, the most hideous yells that can be conceived, are sent forth from at least three score of throats; and Ovids, and Virgils, and Horaces, together with the more heavy metal of dictionaries, whether of Cole, of Young, or of Ainsworth, are hurled without remorse at the head of the astonished preceptor, who, on his side, groping and crawling under cover of the forms, makes the best of his way to the door. When attained, and light restored, a death-like silence ensues. Every boy is at his lesson; no one has had a hand or a voice in the recent atrocity: what then is to be done, and who shall be chastised.

•   •   •

As it frequently happens in human affairs, that men are misplaced, and that those found in a subordinate station are better fitted for the supreme authority than those who are invested with it, so it generally was in the Latin school of the academy. The ushers, during the term of my pupilage, a period of four years or more, were often changed; and some of them, it must be admitted, were insignificant enough: but others, were men of sense and respectability, to whom, on a comparison with the principal, the management of the school might have been committed with much advantage. . . .

With respect to my progress and that of the class to which I belonged, it was reputable and perhaps laudable for the first two years. From a pretty close application, we were well grounded in grammar, and had passed through the elementary books, much to the approbation of our teachers; but at length, with a single exception, we became possessed of the demons of liberty and idleness. We were, to a great degree, impatient of the restraints of a school; and if we yet retained any latent sparks of the emulation of improvement, we were, unfortunately, never favored with the collision that could draw them forth. We could feelingly have exclaimed with Louis the fourteenth, *mais a quoi sert de lire!* but where's the use of all this pouring over books! One boy thought he had Latin enough, as he was not designed for a learned profession; his father thought so too, and was about taking him from school. Another was of opinion that he might be much better employed in a counting-house, and was also about ridding himself of his scholastic shackles. As this was a consummation devoutly wished by us all, we cheerfully renounced the learned professions for the sake of the supposed liberty that would be the consequence. We were all, therefore, to be merchants, as to be mechanics was too humiliating; and accordingly, when the question was proposed, which of us would enter upon the study of Greek, the grammar of which tongue was about to be put into our hands, there were but two or three who declared for it. As to myself, it was my mother's desire, from her knowing it to have been my father's intention to give me the best education the country afforded, that I should go on, and acquire every language and science that was taught in the institution; but, as my evil star would have it, I was thoroughly tired of books and confinement, and her advice and even entreaties were overruled by my extreme repugnance to a longer continuance in the college [i.e., academy], which, to my lasting regret, I bid adieu to when a little turned of fourteen, at the very season when the minds of the studious begin to profit by instruction. We were at this time reading Horace and Cicero, having passed through Ovid, Virgil, Caesar and Sallust. . . .

16.—SELF-EDUCATION

Although many American youths gained valuable training at writing schools and academies, other youths acquired the necessary knowledge in less formal ways—from parents and friends, from practical experience, and from reading widely on their own initiative. Such was the case with Benjamin Franklin. While no one would argue that Franklin was a typical American colonist—he was unusually bright, energetic, and ambitious—his experiences as a youth in Boston and Philadelphia reveal much about the opportunities and limitations of education in Colonial America. The selection below is from his justly famous autobiography.—From John Bigelow, ed., The Life of Benjamin Franklin, Written by Himself *(Philadelphia, 1879), pp. 99-100, 102, 104, 105-113, 156-157, 182-184, 220-221, 223, 255-256.*

My elder brothers were all put apprentices to different trades. I was put to the grammar-school at eight years of age, my father intending to devote me, as the tithe of his sons, to the service of the Church. My early readiness in learning to read (which must have been very early, as I do not remember when I could not read), and the opinion of all his friends, that I should certainly make a good scholar, encouraged him in this purpose of his. My uncle Benjamin, too, approved of it, and proposed to give me all his short-hand volumes of sermons, I suppose as a stock to set up with, if I would learn his character. I continued, however, at the grammar-school not quite one year, though in that time I had risen gradually from the middle of the class of that year to be the head of it, and farther was removed into the next class above it, in order to go with that into the third at the end of the year. But my father, in the mean time, from a view of the expense of a college education, which having so

large a family he could not well afford, and the mean living many
so educated were afterwards able to obtain—reasons that he gave to
his friends in my hearing—altered his first intention, took me from
the grammar-school, and sent me to a school for writing and arithmetic, kept by a then famous man, Mr. George Brownell, very success-
ful in his profession generally, and that by mild, encouraging methods.
Under him I acquired fair writing pretty soon but I failed in the
arithmetic, and made no progress in it At ten years old I was taken
home to assist my father in his business, which was that of a tallow-
chandler and sope-boiler; a business he was not bred to, but had as-
sumed on his arrival in New England, and on finding his dying trade
would not maintain his family, being in little request. Accordingly,
I was employed in cutting wick for the candles, filling the dipping
mold and the molds for cast candles, attending the shop, going of
errands, etc.

• • •

. . . At his table [my father] liked to have, as often as he could,
some sensible friend or neighbor to converse with, and always took
care to start some ingenious or useful topic for discourse, which
might tend to improve the minds of his children. By this means he
turned our attention to what was good, just, and prudent in the conduct of life; and little or no notice was ever taken of what related to
the victuals on the table. . . .

• • •

. . . I continued thus in my father's business for two years, that is,
till I was twelve years old; and my brother John, who was bred to
that business, having left my father, married, and set up for himself
at Rhode Island, there was all appearance that I was destined to
supply his place, and become a tallow-chandler. But my dislike to the
trade continuing, my father was under apprehensions that if he did
not find one for me more agreeable, I should break away and get to
sea, as his son, Josiah had done, to his great vexation. He therefore
sometimes took me to walk with him, and see joiners, bricklayers,
turners, braziers, etc., at their work, that he might observe my inclination, and endeavor to fix it on some trade or other on land. It
has ever since been a pleasure to me to see good workmen handle
their tools; and it has been useful to me, having learnt so much by it
as to be able to do little jobs myself in my house when a workman
could not readily be got, and to construct little machines for my experiments, while the intention of making the experiment was fresh
and warm in my mind. My father at last fixed upon the cutler's
trade, and my uncle Benjamin's son Samuel, who was bred to that

business in London, being about that time established in Boston; I was sent to be with him some time on liking. But his expectations of a fee with me displeasing my father, I was taken home again.

From a child I was fond of reading, and all the little money that came into my hands was ever laid out in books. Pleased with the Pilgrim's Progress, my first collection was of John Bunyan's works in separate little volumes. I afterward sold them to enable me to buy R. Burton's Historical Collections; they were small chapmen's books, and cheap, 40 or 50 in all. My father's little library consisted chiefly of books in polemic divinity, most of which I read, and have since often regretted that, at a time when I had such a thirst for knowledge, more proper books had not fallen in my way, since it was now resolved I should not be a clergyman. Plutarch's Lives there was in which I read abundantly, and I still think that time spent to great advantage. There was also a book of De Foe's, called an Essay on Projects, and another of Dr. Mather's, called Essays to do Good, which perhaps gave me a turn of thinking that had an influence on some of the principal future events of my life.

This bookish inclination at length determined my father to make me a printer, though he had already one son (James) of that profession. In 1717 my brother James returned from England with a press and letters to set up his business in Boston. I liked it much better than that of my father, but still had a hankering for the sea. To prevent the apprehended effect of such an inclination, my father was impatient to have me bound to my brother. I stood out some time, but at last was persuaded, and signed the indentures when I was yet but twelve years old. I was to serve as an apprentice till I was twenty-one years of age, only I was to be allowed journeyman's wages during the last year. In a little time I made great proficiency in the business, and became a useful hand to my brother. I now had access to better books. An acquaintance with the apprentices of booksellers enabled me sometimes to borrow a small one, which I was careful to return soon and clean. Often I sat up in my room reading the greatest part of the night, when the book was borrowed in the evening and to be returned early in the morning, lest it should be missed or wanted.

And after some time an ingenious tradesman, Mr. Matthew Adams, who had a pretty collection of books, and who frequented our printing-house, took notice of me, invited me to his library, and very kindly lent me such books as I chose to read. I now took a fancy to poetry, and made some little pieces; my brother, thinking it might turn to account, encouraged me, and put me on composing occasional ballads. One was called *The Lighthouse Tragedy,* and contained an

account of the drowning of Captain Worthilake, with his two daughters: the other was a sailor's song, on the taking of *Teach* (or Black-
beard) the pirate. They were wretched stuff, in the Grub-street-ballad
style; and when they were printed he sent me about the town to sell
them. The first sold wonderfully, the event being recent, having made
a great noise. This flattered my vanity; but my father discouraged
me by ridiculing my performances, and telling me verse-makers were
generally beggars. So I escaped being a poet, most probably a very
bad one; but as prose writing has been of great use to me in the
course of my life, and was a principal means of my advancement, I
shall tell you how, in such a situation, I acquired what little ability I
have in that way.

There was another bookish lad in the town, John Collins by name,
with whom I was intimately acquainted. We sometimes disputed, and
very fond we were of argument, and very desirous of confuting one
another, which disputatious turn, by the way, is apt to become a very
bad habit, making people often extremely disagreeable in company by
the contradiction that is necessary to bring it into practice; and
thence, besides souring and spoiling the conversation, is productive
of disgusts and, perhaps enmities where you may have occasion for
friendship. I had caught it by reading my father's books of dispute
about religion. Persons of good sense, I have since observed, seldom
fall into it, except lawyers, university men, and men of all sorts that
have been bred at Edinborough.

A question was once, somehow or other, started between Collins
and me, of the propriety of educating the female sex in learning, and
their abilities for study. He was of opinion that it was improper, and
that they were naturally unequal to it. I took the contrary side, perhaps a little for dispute's sake. He was naturally more eloquent, had
a ready plenty of words; and sometimes, as I thought, bore me down
more by his fluency than by the strength of his reasons. As we parted
without settling the point, and were not to see one another again for
some time, I sat down to put my arguments in writing, which I copied
fair and sent to him. He answered, and I replied. Three or four letters of a side had passed, when my father happened to find my papers
and read them. Without entering into the discussion, he took occasion
to talk to me about the manner of my writing; observed that, though
I had the advantage of my antagonist in correct spelling and pointing
(which I ow'd to the printing-house), I fell far short in elegance of
expression, in method and in perspicuity, of which he convinced me
by several instances. I saw the justice of his remarks, and thence

grew more attentive to the manner in writing, and determined to endeavor at improvement.

About this time I met with an odd volume of the *Spectator*. It was the third. I had never before seen any of them. I bought it, read it over and over, and was much delighted with it. I thought the writing excellent, and wished, if possible, to imitate it. With this view I took some of the papers, and, making short hints of the sentiment in each sentence, laid them by a few days, and then, without looking at the book, try'd to compleat the papers again, by expressing each hinted sentiment at length, and as fully as it had been expressed before, in any suitable words that should come to hand. Then I compared my *Spectator* with the original, discovered some of my faults, and corrected them. But I found I wanted a stock of words, or a readiness in recollecting and using them, which I thought I should have acquired before that time if I had gone on making verses; since the continual occasion for words of the same import, but of different length, to suit the measure, or of different sound for the rhyme, would have laid me under a constant necessity of searching for variety, and also have tended to fix that variety in my mind, and make me master of it. Therefore I took some of the tales and turned them into verse; and, after a time, when I had pretty well forgotten the prose, turned them back again. I also sometimes jumbled my collections of hints into confusion, and after some weeks endeavored to reduce them into the best order, before I began to form the full sentences and compleat the paper. This was to teach me method in the arrangement of thoughts. By comparing my work afterwards with the original, I discovered many faults and amended them; but I sometimes had the pleasure of fancying that, in certain particulars of small import, I had been lucky enough to improve the method or the language, and this encouraged me to think I might possibly in time come to be a tolerable English writer, of which I was extreamly ambitious. My time for these exercises and for reading was at night, after work or before it began in the morning, or on Sundays, when I contrived to be in the printing-house alone. . . .

• • •

And now it was that, being on some occasion made asham'd of my ignorance in figures, which I had twice failed in learning when at school, I took Cocker's book of Arithmetick, and went through the whole by myself with great ease. I also read Seller's and Shermy's books of Navigation, and became acquainted with the little geometry they contain; but never proceeded far in that science. And I read about this time Locke *on Human Understanding,* and the *Art of Thinking,* by Messrs. du Port Royal.

While I was intent on improving my language, I met with an English grammar (I think it was Greenwood's), at the end of which there were two little sketches of the arts of rhetoric and logic, the latter finishing with a specimen of a dispute in the Socratic method; and soon after I procur'd Xenophon's Memorable Things of Socrates, wherein there are many instances of the same method. I was charm'd with it, adopted it, dropt my abrupt contradiction and positive argumentation and put on the humble inquirer and doubter. . . .

· · ·

. . . While I lodg'd in Little Britain [during a visit to England in 1724] I made an acquaintance with one Wilcox, a bookseller, whose shop was at the next door. He had an immense collection of second-hand books. Circulating libraries were not then in use; but we agreed that, on certain reasonable terms, which I have now forgotten, I might take, read, and return any of his books. This I esteem'd a great advantage, and I made as much use of it as I could.

My pamphlet by some means falling into the hands of one Lyons, a surgeon, author of a book entitled "The Infallibility of Human Judgment," it occasioned an acquaintance between us. He took great notice of me, called on me often to converse on those subjects, carried me to the Horns, a pale alehouse in —— Lane, Cheapside, and introduced me to Mr. Mandeville, author of the "Fable of the Bees," who had a club there, of which he was the soul, being a most facetious, entertaining companion. Lyons, too, introduced me to Dr. Pemberton, at Batson's Coffee-house, who promis'd to give me an opportunity, some time or other, of seeing Sir Isaac Newton, of which I was extreamely desirous; but this never happened.

· · ·

I should have mentioned before, that, in the autumn of the preceding year [1726], I had form'd most of my ingenious acquaintance into a club of mutual improvement, which we called the JUNTO; we met on Friday evenings. The rules that I drew up required that every member, in his turn, should produce one or more queries on any point of Morals, Politics, or Natural Philosophy, to be discuss'd by the company; and once in three months produce and read an essay of his own writing, on any subject he pleased. Our debates were to be under the direction of a president, and to be conducted in the sincere spirit of inquiry after truth, without fondness for dispute, or desire of victory; and, to prevent warmth, all expressions of positiveness in opinions, or direct contradiction, were after some time made contraband, and prohibited under small pecuniary penalties.

The first members were Joseph Breintnal, a copyer of deeds for the scriveners, a good-natur'd, friendly, middle-ag'd man, a great lover of poetry, reading all he could meet with, and writing some that was tolerable; very ingenious in many little Nicknackeries, and of sensible conversation.

Thomas Godfrey, a self-taught mathematician, great in his way, and afterward inventor of what is now called Hadley's Quadrant. But he knew little out of his way, and was not a pleasing companion; as, like most great mathematicians I have met with, he expected universal precision in every thing said, or was for ever denying or distinguishing upon trifles, to the disturbance of all conversation. He soon left us.

Nicholas Scull, a surveyor, afterward surveyor-general, who lov'd books, and sometimes made a few verses.

William Parsons, bred a shoemaker, but, loving reading, had acquir'd a considerable share of mathematics, which he first studied with a view to astrology, that he afterwards laught at it. He also became surveyor-general.

William Maugridge, a joiner, a most exquisite mechanic, and a solid, sensible man.

Hugh Meredith, Stephen Potts, and George Webb I have characteriz'd before [in a section not reprinted here—ED.].

Robert Grace, a young gentleman of some fortune, generous, lively, and witty; a lover of punning and of his friends.

And William Coleman, then a merchant's clerk, about my age, who had the coolest, clearest head, the best heart, and the exactest morals of almost any man I ever met with. He became afterwards a merchant of great note, and one of our provincial judges. Our friendship continued without interruption to his death, upward of forty years; and the club continued almost as long, and was the best school of philosophy, morality, and politics that then existed in the province; for our queries, which were read the week preceding their discussion, put us upon reading with attention upon the several subjects, that we might speak more to the purpose; and here, too, we acquired better habits of conversation, every thing being studied in our rules which might prevent our disgusting each other. . . .

●   ●   ●

At the time I establish'd myself in Pennsylvania, there was not a good bookseller's shop in any of the colonies to the southward of

Boston. In New York and Philad'a the printers were indeed stationers; they sold only paper, etc., almanacs, ballads, and a few common school-books. Those who lov'd reading were oblig'd to send for their books from England; the members of the Junto had each a few. We had left the alehouse, where we first met, and hired a room to hold our club in. I propos'd that we should all of us bring our books to that room, where they would not only be ready to consult in our conferences, but become a common benefit, each of us being at liberty to borrow such as he wish'd to read at home. This was accordingly done, and for some time contented us.

Finding the advantage of this little collection, I propos'd to render the benefit from books more common, by commencing a public subscription library. . . .

•   •   •

This library afforded me the means of improvement by constant study, for which I set apart an hour or two each day, and thus repair'd in some degree the loss of the learned education my father once intended for me. Reading was the only amusement I allow'd myself. . . .

•   •   •

I had begun in 1733 to study languages; I soon made myself so much a master of the French as to be able to read the books with ease. I then undertook the Italian. An acquaintance, who was also learning it, us'd often to tempt me to play chess with him. Finding this took up too much of the time I had to spare for study, I at length refus'd to play any more, unless on this condition, that the victor in every game should have a right to impose a task, either in parts of the grammar to be got by heart, or in translations, etc., which tasks the vanquish'd was to perform upon honour, before our next meeting. As we play'd pretty equally, we thus beat one another into that language. I afterwards with a little painstaking, acquir'd as much of the Spanish as to read their books also.

I have already mention'd that I had only one year's instruction in a Latin school, and that when very young, after which I neglected that language entirely. But, when I had attained an acquaintance with the French, Italian, and Spanish, I was surpriz'd to find, on looking over a Latin Testament, that I understood so much more of that language than I had imagined, which encouraged me to apply myself again to the study of it, and I met with more success, as those preceding languages had greatly smooth'd my way.

17.—THE PURSUIT
OF USEFUL KNOWLEDGE

During the eighteenth century many Americans sought learning from the myriad of private tutors who thrived in cities and larger towns. At the same time Americans began to demand a less classical content in their public schools. Anyone who read the provincial newspapers saw abundant evidence of both trends. The first item is an anonymous letter to the editor of a New York newspaper; following it are advertisements from several colonial papers.—From originals and photocopies at Columbia University and The New-York Historical Society.

[Letter to the editor of *The New-York Gazette or Weekly Post-Boy,* December 11, 1752]

I am glad to find the publick Attention again drawn to consider the great advantages, which every Country gains by a proper Education of Youth. This has been the principal Care of the Legislators in all well formed Governments, as the most certain means of securing their Liberty, and promoting their Prosperity. Ignorance and Poverty of the comforts of life, in all countries, are constant companions. Parents, in the best form'd republics, were not suffer'd to be indolent in the Education of their children; but were constrain'd, by the laws, to give them some kind of Education, suited to their rank, so as to make them useful members in the Society where they liv'd, to prevent their pursuing idle and vicious courses, by employing them early in some kind of Business or other. In a well constituted Common-wealth, like Bees, no Drones are suffered to live on the industry of others. At present I shall only consider that branch of Education commonly call'd learning, and which is at this time the Subject of publick discourse: tho' I think the early enuring Children to some kind of Labour, or Trade, or Business in general, as necessary for the wellfare of a Country, and the happiness of the children themselves, as any other kind of learning whatsoever.

•　　•　　•

. . . The erecting Schools can be attended with no difficulty, [for] we need only follow the example of a Neighbouring Colony, in obliging the Inhabitants, by Law, to build a School-house in every Precinct or Township, and by an easy tax to give encouragement to a School Master, to teach the children of the poorer sort at a moderate rate. If this were done, persons sufficiently qualified for this purpose can be easily obtain'd.

I expect, that it will be objected, that the teaching of the Greek and Latin Languages are intirely neglected in this Scheme. To which I answer, that I have on purpose neglected them, as no way necessary for the general Education of youth, in any thing necessary for useful knowledge. How many children have been forced to drudge several years in learning Greek and Latin, who after they left the School, entirely forgot those Languages, by their being of no manner of use to them in their course of Life. As to these (who are likewise the most numerous) their time certainly might have been better employ'd, in learning something more useful to them, in their manner of life and business. Greek and Latin were the Languages of the people in Greece and Rome, and no reason can be given why all kind of Learning may not be taught in our Mother Tongue, as well as it was among the Grecians and Romans in theirs. When Learning began to revive first in Europe, at the Reformation, all the Books of Learning were in Greek and Latin, and therefore those Languages were then previously necessary to Learning; but it is otherwise now, we have Books in English sufficient for instruction, in every part of a genteel Education, and of generally useful Knowledge. I would not however be understood by this, as that I intended to banish the Greek and Latin Languages from the Schools. No, but I think them only useful for such as intend to make the learned Sciences the employment of their lives in the Study of Divinity, Law, or Physicks; and one School of Greek and Latin, at New York, will in our present circumstances, and for some years, be sufficient for these purposes. . . .

[From the *Pennsylvania Gazette*, August 2, 1759]

Philadelphia, July 27, 1759

WHEREAS Mr. David James Dove, late master of a public Grammar School, in this City, finding his State of Health so far reduced, as to render him incapable of taking upon him the Charge of the many Scholars he has hitherto been favoured with, has thought fit to make me the Offer of being chief Master in his Stead, I therefore take this Opportunity to inform the Public, that on Monday the 30th Instant my School will be open, where he lately kept his. Gentlemen and Ladies who are pleased to favour me with their Children, may have them carefully instructed in the following Manner, viz.

1. Children, who have not yet learned the Elements of their Mother Tongue, will be taught expeditiously by me to pronounce, spell, and read properly, in a Manner most easy to themselves.

2. Young Gentlemen, who have made any tolerable Progress in the English Language, will be taught the Art of fair Writing, Merchants Accounts, and a grammatical Knowledge of their Mother Tongue, as it is judiciously laid down in Greenwood's English Grammar.

3. A compendious System of practical Mathematics, consisting of some Books of the Elements of Euclid, Trigonometry, and practical Geometry.

4. The Knowledge of the Greek and Latin Tongues, including the most valuable Authors of the Roman Classics.

5. And lastly, the following Sciences, namely, Geography, Rhetoric, Poetry, History, Moral Philosophy, and Physics.

SIMON WILLIAMS.

N. B. *As I am in a Manner a Stranger in this Place, I beg Leave to inform the Public, that James Spence, Esq; is now residing in this City. He is a Gentleman of Fortune and approved Integrity, who lately came from Jamaica, where I kept a public School. He will give any Gentleman sufficient Satisfaction concerning my moral Conduct while I followed the Profession in that Colony.*

*** Twelve Shillings and Six pence per Quarter, for Reading and Writing; and Five Shillings Entrance. Twenty Shillings per Quarter for the rest, and Twenty Shillings Entrance.

[From the *Boston Evening Post*, November 28, 1737]

At the North End of *Boston*, in the Fore Street, near the Sign of the *Red Lyon*, are taught these Mathematical Sciences, *viz. Arithmetick, Geometry, Algebra, Fluxions, Trigonometry, Navigation, Dialing, Astronomy, Surveying, Gauging, Fortification, Gunnery; the Use of the Globes, also other Mathematical Instruments, like-*

wise the Projecting of the Sphere on any Circle, etc. with other parts of the Mathematicks.

By Samuel Scammell,
*Formerly a Teacher of the Gentlemen Volunteers
in His Majesty's Royal Navy.*

৵

[From *The Maryland Gazette*, December 13, 1759]

At LOWER-MARLBOROUGH *in* Calvert *County,*

YOUTH are TAUGHT, after an entire new and most expeditious Method, ENGLISH, FRENCH, LATIN, GREEK, HEBREW, PRINT-HAND, ROMAN and ITALIC, the several approved WRITING-HANDS, SHORT-HAND, ARITHMETIC, etc. etc.

By R. PHILIPSON, a MASTER of LANGUAGES.

For *English, Latin, Greek,* Common Writing, and Arithmetic, One Guinea Entrance, and Six Guineas *per Annum.*

For *English,* Common Writing and Arithmetic, One Pistole Entrance, and Four Pounds Sterling *per Annum.*

For Short-Hand, One Guinea Entrance, Two Guineas *per* Month, One Hour a Day Attendance.

N. B. The Short-Hand is remarkable for Simplicity.

Regard is likewise had to the Morals of Youth, and Care taken to blend in such as are proper Subjects, the Materials for constructing the admired, though not very common Character, the GENTLEMAN and CHRISTIAN together.

৵

[From *The Maryland Gazette*, August 11, 1757]

Annapolis, August 4, 1757.

The Subscriber intends to open a DANCING SCHOOL at Annapolis the Nineteenth Instant, to be Taught every Friday and Saturday, for Six Pounds a Year, and a Pistole Entrance: And those who chuse to learn by the Quarter, to pay Forty Shillings and the Entrance.

As the principal Gentlemen and Ladies at *Annapolis,* have subscribed to send their Children to the Dancing-School, the Subscriber hopes the Gentlemen and Ladies in the Neighbourhood, will follow their Example.

JOHN ORMSBY

N. B. The Subscriber intends to Teach DANCING Two Days in the Week at Baltimore-Town or Upper-Marlborough, about the latter End of this Month. He also Teaches the Noble Science of DEFENCE, at a reasonable Rate.

18.—GENESIS

OF A COLONIAL COLLEGE

The New York newspapers in the 1750s carried frequent articles concerning a new college—referred to at first as the College of New York, officially opened in 1754 as King's College, and renamed Columbia College in 1776. Printed here is the first president's appeal for students.—From a copy at The New-York Historical Society.

[From *The New-York Gazette or Weekly Post-Boy,* June 3, 1754]

May 31, 1754

Advertisement.

To such Parents as have now (or expect to have) Children prepared to be educated in the College of New-York.

I. As the Gentlemen who are appointed by the Assembly, to be Trustees of the intended Seminary or College of *New-York,* have thought fit to appoint me to take the Charge of it, and have concluded to set up a Course of Tuition in the learned Languages, and in the liberal Arts and Sciences: They have judged it advisable, that I should publish this *Advertisement,* to inform such as have Children ready for a College Education, that it is proposed to begin Tuition upon the first Day of *July* next, at the *Vestry Room* in the new *School-House,* adjoining to *Trinity Church* in *New-York,* which the Gentlemen of the Vestry are so good as to favour them with the Use of in the Interim, till a convenient Place may be built.

II. The lowest Qualifications they have judged requisite, in order to Admission into the said College, are as follow, *viz.* That they be able to read well, and write a good legible Hand; and that they be well versed in the Five first Rules in *Arithmetic,* i.e. as far as *Division* and *Reduction;* and as to *Latin* and *Greek,* That they have a good Knowledge in the *Grammars,* and be able to make grammatical *Latin,* and both in construing and parsing, to give a good Account of two or three of the first select Orations of *Tully,* and of the first Books of *Virgil's Aeneid,* and some of the first Chapters of the *Gospel* of St. *John,* in *Greek.* In these Books therefore they may expect to be examined; but higher Qualifications must hereafter be expected: and if there be any of the higher Classes in any College, or under private Instruction, that incline to come hither, they may expect Admission to proportionably higher Classes here.

III. And that People may be the better satisfied in sending their Children for Education to this College, it is to be understood, that as to Religion, there is no Intention to impose on the Schollars, the peculiar Tenets of any particular Sect of Christians; but to inculcate upon their tender Minds, the great Principles of Christianity and Morality, in which true Christians of each Denomination are generally agreed. And as to the daily Worship in the College Morning and Evening, it is proposed that it should, ordinarily, consist of such a Collection of Lessons, Prayers and Praises of the Liturgy of the Church, as are, for the most Part, taken out of the Holy Scriptures, and such as are agreed on by the Trustees, to be in the best Manner expressive of our common Christianity; and, as to any peculiar Tenets, every one is left to judge freely for himself, and to be required only to attend constantly at such Places of Worship, on the Lord's Day, as their Parents or Guardians shall think fit to order or permit.

IV. The chief Thing that is aimed at in this College is, to teach and engage the Children to *know God in Jesus Christ,* and to love and serve him, in all *Sobriety, Godliness* and *Righteousness* of Life, with *a perfect Heart, and a willing Mind;* and to train them up in all virtuous Habits, and all such useful Knowledge as may render them creditable to their Families and Friends, Ornaments to their Country, and useful to the public Weal in their Generations. To which good Purposes, it is earnestly desired, that their Parents, Guardians and Masters, would train them up from their Cradles, under strict Government, and in all Seriousness, Virtue and Industry, that they may be qualified to make orderly and tractable Members of this Society;—and, above all, that in order hereunto, they be very careful themselves, to set them good Examples of true Piety and Virtue in their own Conduct. For as Examples have a very powerful Influence over young Minds, and especially those of their Parents, in vain are they solicitous for a good Education for their Children, if they themselves set before them Examples of Impiety and Profanness, or of any sort of Vice whatsoever.

V. And, *lastly*, a serious, *virtuous*, and *industrious* Course of Life, being first provided for, it is further the Design of this College, to instruct and perfect the Youth in the learned Languages, and in the Arts of *reasoning* exactly, of *writing* correctly, and *speaking* eloquently; and in the Arts of *numbering* and *measuring; of Surveying* and *Navigation*, of *Geography* and *History*, of *Husbandry, Commerce* and *Government*, and in the Knowledge of *all Nature* in the *Heavens* above us, and in the *Air, Water* and *Earth* around us, and the various kinds of *Meteors, Stones, Mines* and *Minerals, Plants* and *Animals*, and of every Thing *useful* for the Comfort, the Convenience and Elegance of Life, in the chief *Manufactures* relating to any of these Things: And, finally, to lead them from the Study of Nature to the Knowledge of themselves, and of the God of Nature, and their Duty to him, themselves, and one another, and every Thing that can contribute to their true Happiness, both here and hereafter.

Thus much, *Gentlemen*, it was thought proper to advertise you of, concerning the Nature and Design of this College: And I pray GOD, it may be attended with all the Success you can wish, for the best Good of the rising Generations; to which, (while I continue here) I shall willingly contribute my Endeavours to the Utmost of my Power,

> *Who am, Gentlemen,*
> *Your real Friend,*
> *And most humble Servant,*
> SAMUEL JOHNSON.

N. B. *The Charge of the Tuition is established by the Trustees to be only 25s. for each Quarter.*

19.—COLLEGE LIFE

Shortly after his arrival at the College of New Jersey, later Princeton University, Philip Vickers Fithian de-

scribed to his father the life of a freshman in a provincial
college.—From John Rogers Williams, ed., Philip Vickers
Fithian: Journal and Letters, 1767-1774 *(Princeton, 1900),*
pp. 6-10.

Written at Nassau Hall,
in Princeton Novem: 30th Anno 1770.

Very Dear Father.

Altho' I am very busy seeing I begun to study three Weeks later
than the rest of our Class, yet I think it my Duty to give you Notice
of my Admission to this flourishing *Seminary* of Learning, which is
another grand Step towards the Summit of my Wishes; And I shall
also mention as many of the Customs, as my short Acquaintance with
the College & Students will allow me, & as any thing new occurs
shall not fail at any time to transmit it.

Mr. [Andrew] *Hunter* and myself, were admitted into the junior-
Class on the twenty second day of November, after a previous Examination by the president, Tutors, & some residing Graduates; Which
was about three Weeks after the College-Orders began.

The Rules by which the Scholars & Students are directed, are, in
my Opinion, exceedingly well formed to check & restrain the vicious,
& to assist the studious, & to countenance & incourage the virtuous.

Every Student must rise in the Morning, at farthest by half an
hour after five; the grammar Schollars being most of them small, &
lodging also in Town at some Distance from the College, are, in
Winter, excused from attending morning Prayrs.

The Bell rings at five, after which there is an Intermission of half
and hour, that everyone may have time to dress, at the end of which
it rings again, & Prayrs begin; And lest any should plead that he
did not hear the Bell, the Servant who rings, goes to every Door &
beats till he wakens the Boys, which leaves them without Excuse.

There are Bill-keepers in each Class, appointed generally by the
President, or in his absence by one of the Tutors, who take Notice,
& set down those who are absent from Morning or evening Prayrs,
& once every week present their Bill to the *Doctor,* or one of the
Tutors, who call each delinquent, & demand their Excuse, which if
it is thought sufficeant is accepted, if not they are fined, or privately
admonished, & if the same person is found frequently guilty, without
good reason, he receives public Admonition in the Hall for Contempt of Authority.

After morning Prayrs, we can, now in the Winter, study an hour by candle Light every Morning.

We breakfast at eight; from Eight to nine, is time of our own, to play, or exercise.

At nine the Bell rings for Recitation, after which we study till one, when the Bell rings for Dinner—We dine all in the same Room, at three Tables, & so we breakfast and sup:

After dinner till three we have Liberty to go out at Pleasure.

From three til' five we study, when the Bell rings for evening Prayrs.

We sup at seven; At nine the Bell rings for Study; And a Tutor goes through College, to see that every Student is in his own Room; if he finds that any are absent, or more in any Room than belongs there, he notes them down, & the day following calls them to an Account.

After nine any may go to bed, but to go before is reproachful.

No Student is allowed, on any pretence, Sickness only excepted, to be absent on Sunday, from public Worship: We have two Sermons every Sabbath: One at eleven in the morning, in the Church; & the other at three in the Afternoon, in the College Hall. I am indeed much pleased with Dr. *Witherspoon* [president of the College] & think his Sermons almost inimitable.

We rise on Sabbath mornings & have Prayrs as usual,

There is a Society that meets every Sabbath Evening at six o Clock, for religious Worship; this is a voluntary Society made up of any who belong to the College, & choose to attend.

The Exercises in this Society go in the alphebetical Order of those who are willing to perform: They sing a Psalm & pray, after which a Tutor reads a Sermon & dismisses them.

About seven the supper Bell rings, immediately after which, each Class meets separately in Rooms belonging to one of themselves; The Seniors alone meet in a Room belonging to one of the Seniors; & the Juniors by themselves meet in a Room belonging to one of themselves; & in like manner do the inferior Classes. And one in each Class, as his Name comes in alphebetical Order, gives out a Psalm to be sung, & prays; after which they disperse, and retire to their respective Rooms.

I make use of the word "their" not because I do not join with my fellow-Students in these Acts of Worship, but because I seem only yet to be an Observer of their Manners.

There are upwards of an hundred now in the College including the grammar Scholars: The present Senior Class consists of ten: the

Junior of twenty-eight: The *Sophimore* of twenty five: And the *Freshman* of eighteen: In the School there are about twenty-five.

I am, through divine goodness, very well, & more reconciled to rising in the Morning so early than at first.

•   •   •

Please to accept my humble, & sincere Regard; & give my kindest Love to my ever-dear *Mamma.*

From, Sir, your dutiful Son

P. FITHIAN

V

This World
and the Next

In the seventeenth century, one of the avowed purposes of education in America—indeed of new settlement itself—had been the preservation and propagation of Christianity. At the same time bitter denominational rivalry characterized the religious ardor of the early colonists, making matters of theological doctrine, ecclesiastical organization, and church privilege grist for endless individual and community strife. By contrast, eighteenth-century America witnessed little religious animosity. Gone was the religious exclusiveness of the previous century, when each sect carved out a community for itself and asked people of different theologies to settle elsewhere. Gone too was the conviction that toleration of religious dissent meant disloyalty to God.

By the middle of the eighteenth century the American colonist was confronted with a confusing variety of faiths, as wave after wave of immigrants brought new forms of religion to the American shore. At the same time, rifts within the older churches—especially during the "Great Awakening" of 1720-1760—gave birth to additional sects. And accompanying this proliferation came toleration, a force that had grown steadily in America ever since the Civil Wars in England had demonstrated the impracticality of religious strife. Not surprisingly, then, Philadelphia in 1750 could boast of ten denominations, each with enough members to support one or more church buildings of their own; while Boston, though still predominantly Congregational Puritan, had enclaves of Presbyterians, Episcopalians, Baptists, Quakers, and Huguenots. Only the persistence of established churches—that is, churches supported by civil authorities—in some of the colonies serves as a reminder that full religious equality —as distinct from religious toleration—was still in the future.

Paralleling Colonial America's growing denominational fragmentation and consequent toleration was the emergence of two contradictory but typically American characteristics: religious enthusiasm and religious indifference. The former found manifestation in the Great Awakening; the latter revealed itself in the decline of church attendance (especially on the frontier), the gradual lessening of clerical prestige, a rising demand for separation of church and state, and an increasing interest in the teachings and spirit of the Enlightenment. But to the eyewitness observer it was apparent that religion —in both its individual and institutional forms—remained a major force in colonial society, and that eighteenth-century Americans were only slightly less interested than their seventeenth-century predecessors had been in the condition of their souls in this world and the next.

20.—A VARIETY OF FAITHS

Probably the most striking feature of religion in Colonial America was its multiplicity of forms. The first part of the selection below consists of the observations of Peter Kalm, a Swedish naturalist who toured the colonies from 1748 to 1751 and noted the denominational variety in Philadelphia. Philadelphia also held a small Jewish community which Kalm did not mention because at that time it had no synagogue. However, the Jews of Newport, Rhode Island, had erected one nearly a century before. In 1763 they built a new synagogue whose opening is described below by Ezra Stiles, Congregational clergyman and later president of Yale.—From Peter Kalm, Travels into North America . . . , *I (Warrington, England, 1770), 36-43; and from Franklin B. Dexter, ed.,* The Literary Diary of Ezra Stiles, *I (New York, 1901), 6.*

[Kalm]

Among the publick buildings I will first mention churches, of which there are several, for God is served in various ways in this country.

1. The *English established church* stands in the northern part of the town, at some distance from the market, and is the finest of all. It has a little, inconsiderable steeple, in which is a bell to be rung when it is time to go to church, and on burials. It has likewise a clock which strikes the hours. This building which is called Christ church, was founded towards the end of the last century, but has lately been rebuilt and more adorned. It has two ministers whc get the greatest part of their salary from *England*. In the beginning of this century, the *Swedish* minister the Rev. Mr. *Rudmann,* performed the functions of a clergyman to the *English* congregation for near two years, during the absence of their own clergyman.

2. The *Swedish church,* which is otherwise called the church of *Weekacko,* is on the southern part of the town, and almost without it, on the river's side, and its situation is therefore more agreeable than that of any other. . . .

3. The *German Lutheran church,* is on the north-west side of the town. On my arrival in *America* it had a little steeple, but that being put up by an ignorant architect, before the walls of the church were quite dry, they leaned forwards by its weight, and therefore they were forced to pull it down again in the autumn of the year 1750. About that time the congregation received a fine organ from *Germany*. They have only one minister, who likewise preaches at another Lutheran church in *Germantown*. He preaches alternately one Sunday in that church, and another in this. The first clergyman which the Lutherans had in this town, was the Rev. Mr. *Muhlenberg,* who laid the foundations of this church in 1743, and being called to another place afterwards, the rev. Mr. *Brunholz* from *Sleswick* was his successor, and is yet here. Both these gentlemen were sent to this place from *Hall* in *Saxony,* and have been a great advantage to it by their peculiar talent of preaching in an edifying manner. A little while before this church was built, the *Lutheran Germans* had no clergyman for themselves, so that the every-where beloved *Swedish* minister at *Weekacko,* Mr. *Dylander,* preached likewise to them. He therefore preached three sermons every sunday; the first early in the morning to the *Germans;* the second to the *Swedes,* and the third in the afternoon to the *English,* and besides this he went all the week into the country and instructed the *Germans* who lived separately there. He therefore frequently preached sixteen sermons a week. And after his death, which happened in *November* 1741, the *Germans* first wrote to *Germany* for a clergyman for themselves. This congregation is at present very numerous, so that every sunday the church is very much crowded. It has two galleries, but no vestry.

They do not sing the collects [short prayer made while congregation is gathering for service], but read them before the altar.

4. The *old Presbyterian church,* is not far from the market, and on the south-side of *market-street.* It is of a middling size, and built in the year 1704, as the inscription on the northern pediment shews. The roof is built almost hemispherical, or at least forms a hexagon. The whole building stands from north to south, for the presbyterians do not regard, as other people do, whether their churches look towards a certain point of the heavens or not.

5. The *new Presbyterian church* was built in the year 1750, by the *New-lights* in the north-western part of the town. By the name of *New-lights,* are understood the people who have, from different religions, become proselytes to the well known *Whitefield,* who in the years 1739, 1740, and likewise in 1744 and 1745 travelled through almost all the *English* colonies. His delivery, his extraordinary zeal, and other talents so well adapted to the intelects of his hearers, made him so popular that he frequently, especially in the two first years, got from eight thousand to twenty thousand hearers in the fields. His intention in these travels, was to collect money for an orphans hospital which had been erected in *Georgia.* He here frequently collected seventy pounds sterling at one sermon; nay, at two sermons which he preached in the year 1740, both on one sunday, at *Philadelphia,* he got an hundred and fifty pounds. The proselytes of this man, or the above-mentioned *new-lights,* are at present merely a sect of presbyterians. For though *Whitefield* was originally a clergyman of the *English* church, yet he deviated by little and little from her doctrines; and on arriving in the year 1744 at *Boston* in *New England,* he disputed with the Presbyterians about their doctrines, so much that he almost entirely embraced them. For *Whitefield* was no great disputant, and could therefore easily be led by these cunning people, withersoever they would have him. This likewise during his latter stay in *America* caused his audience to be less numerous than during the first. The *new-lights* built first in the year 1741, a great house in the western part of the town, to hold divine service in. But a division arising amongst them after the departure of *Whitefield,* and besides on other accounts, the building was sold to the town in the beginning of the year 1750, and destined for a school. The *new-lights* then built a church which I call the *new Presbyterian* one. . . .

6. The *old German reformed church* is built in the west north-west part of the town, and looks like the church in the *Ladugoordfield* near *Stockholm.* It is not yet finished, though for several years together,

the congregation has kept up divine service in it. These *Germans* attended the *German* service at the *Swedish* church, whilst the *Swedish* minister Mr. *Dylander* lived.—But as the *Lutherans* got a clergyman for themselves on the death of the last, those of the reformed church made likewise preparations to get one from *Dordrecht;* and the first who was sent to them, was the Rev. Mr. *Slaughter,* whom I found on my arrival. But in the year 1750, another clergyman of the reformed church arrived from *Holland,* and by his artful behaviour, so insinuated himself into the favour of the Rev. Mr. *Slaughter's* congregation, that the latter lost almost half his audience. The two clergymen then disputed for several sundays together, about the pulpit, nay, people relate that the new comer mounted the pulpit on a saturday, and stayed in it all night. The other being thus excluded, the two parties in the audience, made themselves the subject both of the laughter and of the scorn of the whole town, by beating and bruising each other, and committing other excesses. The affair was inquired into by the magistrates, and decided in favour of the rev. Mr. *Slaughter,* the person who had been abused.

7. The *new reformed church,* was built at a little distance from the old one by the party of the clergyman, who had lost his cause. This man however had influence enough to bring over to his party almost the whole audience of his antagonist, at the end of the year 1750, and therefore this new church will soon be useless.

8. 9. The *Quakers* have two meetings, one in the market, and the other in the northern part of the town. In them are according to the custom of this people, neither altars, nor pulpits, nor any other ornaments usual in churches; but only seats and some sconces. They meet thrice every sunday in them, and besides that at certain times every week or every month. . . .

10. The *Baptists,* have their service, in the northern part of the town.

11. The *Roman Catholicks,* have in the south-west part of the town a great house, which is well adorned within, and has an organ.

12. The *Moravian Brethren,* have hired a great house, in the northern part of the town, in which they performed the service both in *German* and in *English;* not only twice or three times every sunday, but likewise every night after it was grown dark. But in the winter of the year 1750, they were obliged to drop their evening meetings; some wanton young fellows having several times disturbed the congregation, by an instrument sounding like the note of a cuckoo, for this noise they made in a dark corner, not only at the

end of every stanza, but likewise at that of every line, whilst they were singing a hymn.

[Stiles]

Dec. 2, 1763, Friday. In the Afternoon was the dedication of the new Synagogue in this Town. It began by a handsome procession in which were carried the Books of the Law, to be deposited in the Ark. Several Portions of Scripture, & of their Service with a Prayer for the Royal Family, were read and finely sung by the priest & People. There were present many Gentlemen & Ladies. The Order and Decorum, the Harmony & Solemnity of the Musick, together with a handsome Assembly of People, in a Edifice the most perfect of the Temple kind perhaps in America, & splendidly illuminated, could not but raise in the Mind a faint Idea of the Majesty & Grandeur of the Ancient Jewish Worship mentioned in Scripture.

Dr. Isaac de Abraham Touro performed the Service. The Synagogue is about perhaps fourty foot long & 30 wide, of Brick on a Foundation of free Stone: it was begun about two years ago, & is now finished except the Porch & the Capitals of the Pillars. The Front representation of the holy of holies, or its Partition Veil, consists only of wainscotted Breast Work on the East End, in the lower part of which four long Doors cover an upright Square Closet the depth of which is about a foot or the thickness of the Wall, & in this Apartment (vulgarly called the Ark) were deposited three Copies & Rolls of the Pentateuch, written on Vellum or rather tanned Calf Skin: one of these Rolls I was told by Dr. Touro was presented from Amsterdam & is Two Hundred years old; the Letters have the Rabbinical Flourishes.

A Gallery for the Women runs round the whole Inside, except the East End, supported by Columns of Ionic order, over which are placed correspondent Columns of the Corinthian order supporting the Cieling of the Roof. The Depth of the Corinthian Pedestal is the height of the Balustrade which runs round the Gallery. The Pulpit for Reading the Law, is a raised Pew with an extended front table; this placed about the center of the Synagogue or nearer the West End, being a Square embalustraded Comporting with the Length of the indented Chancel before & at the Foot of the Ark.

On the middle of the North Side & affixed to the Wall is a raised Seat for the Parnas or Ruler, & for the Elders; the Breast and Back

interlaid with Chinese Mosaic Work. A Wainscotted Seat runs round
— Sides of the Synagogue below, & another in the Gallery. There are
no other Seats or pews. There may be Eighty Souls of Jews or 15
families now in Town. The synagogue has already cost Fifteen Hundred Pounds Sterling. There are to be five Lamps pendant from a
lofty Ceiling.

21.—ESTABLISHED RELIGION

*Although religious variety was characteristic of eighteenth-
century America, the old notion of a single "official" church
had not entirely expired. In most of the colonies the dominant church—Congregational in New England, Episcopal
in the South—enjoyed special privileges, especially in the
form of public tax-support. In 1770 William Eddis, a royal
official in Maryland, described the position of the Church
of England in his colony.—From William Eddis, Letters
from America (London, 1792), pp. 45-51.*

Annapolis, April 2, 1770

I have previously observed, that Maryland was originally settled
by a colony of Roman Catholicks, who emigrated from Ireland early
in the last century, under the patronage of the then Lord Baltimore.
For some time the inhabitants of that persuasion maintained the
entire ascendancy; but their numbers are at present very inconsiderable, and their influence of no weight in the public concerns of the
province. They, however, continue to be tolerated, without being
permitted to participate in the offices of government. The established
religion is that of the church of England, the members of which communion very greatly exceed the aggregate body of the dissenters of
every denomination.

The province is divided into forty-four parishes, many of which
are populous and extensive. The patronage is solely vested in the
governor, who is thereby enabled to provide, in an ample manner,
for many worthy and respectable characters; and when all circumstances are taken into consideration, the clergy in this part of the
world, will be found to possess advantages greatly superior to the

generality of their brethren in the mother country. Pluralities have never been admitted, the colonists being universally prepossessed against that practice; and to attempt such an innovation, would excite ferments of a dangerous nature. Each incumbent has a neat and convenient habitation, with a sufficient quantity of land, in proper cultivation to answer every useful and domestic purpose; and the emoluments arising from the least beneficial preferment, are amply sufficient to support an appearance, perfectly consistent with the respectability of the clerical profession. The holders of church benefices are also happily exempted from the frequent altercations, which unavoidably take place in the mother country, on account of the collection of tythes.

By the laws of this province, all public dues are levied by a poll-tax. The clergy, from this provision, are entitled to forty pounds of Tobacco for every person within a limited age, at the rate of twelve shillings and six-pence the hundred weight. Persons who plant Tobacco have it in their option to pay either in money or in produce; those who do not, are constantly assessed in specie. A list of the taxables, properly authenticated, is delivered to the sheriff of each county, who collects the clerical revenues, with other public claims; and deducting a moderate commission for transacting this concern, the residue is paid with regularity and dispatch, to the respective incumbents.

As the emoluments of benefices increase, in proportion to the increase of inhabitants, many benefices in this government are rapidly advancing in value, and must, before many years elapse, very greatly exceed the present annual amount. Frederick County, which is considerably the most extensive in this province, in its present state, is only divided into two parishes, one of which, denominated All Saints, I am credibly informed is, at this period, estimated at full one thousand pounds sterling, *per annum;* and from the great increase of population, which is daily taking place in that beautiful and fertile country, it will, very probably, soon produce an income little inferior to many English bishopricks.

I cannot conceive on what principle the colonists are so strongly prejudiced against the introduction of the episcopal order; such an establishment would assuredly be attended with many local advantages, and save much trouble and expense to gentlemen educated in America for the sacred function, who, on the present system, are under the necessity of taking a voyage to England for the purpose of ordination. Throughout the southern provinces, the members of the established church greatly exceed those of all other denominations; yet I am persuaded, any attempt to establish an hierarchy, would be resisted with as much acrimony as during the gloomy prevalence of puritanical zeal. This spirit of opposition, to a measure so evidently conducive to the general good, is the most extraordinary, as the inhabitants of this part of America discover, on every possible occasion, an enlarged and liberal disposition. They have, however, conceived such rooted prejudices against the higher orders of the church, that they are positively persuaded the advantages to be acquired, by such an institution in the colonies, would by no means counter-balance the evils which might arise from it.

22.—REMNANTS
OF INTOLERANCE

By mid-eighteenth century most religious sects, including the established churches, had developed an attitude of "Live and let live" toward rival sects. But as late as the 1760s Anglican clergyman Charles Woodmason discovered bitter intolerance still lingering on the Carolina frontier. At the same time, Ezra Stiles, as the second part of this selection reveals, observed legal and popular harassment of the Jews at Newport.—From Charles Woodmason, The Carolina Backcountry on the Eve of the Revolution, *ed. Richard J. Hooker (Chapel Hill, 1953), pp. 16-18, 30-32, 34, 41-46; and from Franklin B. Dexter, ed.,* The Literary Diary of Ezra Stiles, *I (New York, 1901), 52-53.*

[Woodmason]

[*Feb. 19, 1767*]. I had appointed a Congregation to meet me at the Head of Hanging Rock Creek—Where I arriv'd on Tuesday Evening—Found the Houses filled with debauch'd licentious fellows, and Scot Presbyterians who had hir'd these lawless Ruffians to insult me, which they did with Impunity—Telling me, they wanted no D——d Black Gown Sons of Bitches among them—and threatning to lay me behind the Fire, which they assuredly would have done had not some travellers alighted very opportunely, and taken me under Protection—These Men sat up with, and guarded me all the Night

—In the Morning the lawless Rabble moved off on seeing the Church People appear, of whom had a large Congregation. But the Service was greatly interrupted by a Gang of Presbyterians who kept hallooing and whooping without Door like Indians.—[This concluded a journey of] 30 [miles]

From this Place I went upwards to Cane Creek where I had wrote to the Church People for to assemble—But when I came I found that all my Letters and Advertisements had been intercepted. I trac'd them into the hands of one John Gaston, an Irish Presbyterian Justice of Peace on Fishing Creek, on other Side the River. However, at a Days Notice, about 80 Church People were brought together on Sunday the 27th who behav'd very decently and orderly. One Elderly Gentleman stood Clerk—He brought 6 Sons and 4 Daughters with Him, all excellent Singers, so that the Service was regularly perform'd—Baptiz'd 27 Children.—20 [miles]

•   •   •

In my Absence, found that my Lod[g]ings had been robbed. About 30 Volumes of my Books—much Linen, my Letter folder Port Folio, Key of Desk, and many little Articles taken away. It appear'd to me that Search had been made after my private Papers—and MSS. But they were secur'd. This was some Device of the Presbyterians. By their hurry, they took what Books they first laid hands on, whereby several of my Setts are spoiled.

•   •   •

This Day [Dec. 22(?), 1767] we had another Specimen of the Envy Malice and Temper of the Presbyterians—They gave away 2 Barrels of Whisky to the Populace to make drink, and for to disturb the Service—for this being the 1st time that the Communion was ever celebrated in this Wild remote Part of the World, it gave a Great Alarm, and caus'd them much Pain and Vexation. The Company got drunk by 10 oth Clock and we could hear them firing, hooping, and hallowing like Indians. Some few came before the Communion was finish'd and were very Noisy—and could I have found out the Individuals, would have punish'd them.—837 [total miles]

They took another Step to interrupt the Service of the Day. The Captain of the Corps of Militia on this Creek being a Presbyterian, order'd the Company to appear as this day under Arms to Muster —The Church People refus'd. He threatn'd to fine—They defy'd Him: And had he attempted it, a Battle would certainly have ensu'd in the Muster field between the Church folks and Presbyterians, and Blood been spilt—His Aprehension of Danger to his person made him defer it till the 26th.

Some of the New Lights and Baptists would have communicated as to day, but I did not approve it, till I knew them better—had some proofs of their Sincerity, and could judge whether Motives of Curiosity, not Religion, prompted them.

Cross'd the Country, and the Wateree River to Rocky Mount—was in Great Danger of my Life—the Stream being so rapid that it carried away the Boat down the River and stove us on the Rocks—We threw the Horses over, and they swam to shore and we were taken out by Canoos that came off. I was quite spent with Toil and Sweat—Wet to the Skin, and all my Linen and Baggage soak'd in Water.—25 [miles] ; 862 [total miles]

December 27. Officiated at Rocky Mount. Had but a small Congregation and 5 Communicants—The Name of the Holy Sacrament frightened them all away. Returned with the Church Warden down the Country.—33 [miles]

1768 [January 1]. Preached at Granny Quarter Creek to a mix'd Multitude of People from various Quarters—But no bringing of this Tribe into any Order. They are the lowest Pack of Wretches my Eyes ever saw, or that I have met with in these Woods—As wild as the very Deer—No making of them sit still during Service—but they will be in and out—forward and backward the whole Time (Women especially) as Bees to and fro to their Hives—All this must be born with at the beginning of Things—Nor can be mended till Churches are built, and the Country reduc'd to some Form. How would the Polite People of London stare, to see the Females (many very pretty) come to Service in their Shifts and a short petticoat only, barefooted and Bare legged—Without Caps or Handkerchiefs —dress'd only in their Hair, Quite in a State of Nature for Nakedness is counted as Nothing—as they sleep altogether in Common in one Room, and shift and dress openly without Ceremony—The Men appear in Frocks or Shirts and long Trousers—No Shoes or Stockings—But I should remember that I am talking of my Self, and Religious Matters, Not the Customs of the Country.—36 [miles]

• • •

[April 7, 1768]. In the Morning I sat off, the Weather being fair. Call'd at several Houses to hire Guides and paid them—but they no sooner found that I was a Church [of England] Minister than they quitted me—I hir'd 3 or 4 in this Manner—What was still worse, they would direct me wrong, and send me quite out of the Way—I learn'd however, that there was a rich Man among them, who had plenty of Corn fodder, Meat, Liquors and Necessaries, and that he kept Tavern. I Procur'd a Boy to conduct me, and got there after

riding 30 Miles instead of 12. I found many People there. When I told my Necessity—how sick I was with long fasting—Horse jaded and tir'd—My Self Weary and faint thro' fatigue and Cold, and took out Money to desire Refreshments He would not comply nor sell me a Blade of fodder, a Glass of Liquor (tho' he own'd he had 2 Barrels of Rum in House) nor permit me to sit down nor kindle up a Fire —All my arguments were in vain. He looked on me as an Wolf strayed into Christs fold to devour the Lambs of Grace. Thus did this rigid Presbyterian treat me. At length I got a little Indian Corn for my Horse paying treble Price. Such was the Honesty of the Saint.—30 [miles] ; 1557 [total miles] . . .

• • •

. . . [*June 1768*]. You must understand that all (or greatest Part) of this Part of the Province w[h]ere I am, has been settled within these 5 Years by Irish Presbyterians from Belfast, or Pensylvania and they imagin'd that they could secure this large Tract of fine Country to themselves and their Sect. Hereon, they built Meeting Houses, and got Pastors from Ireland, and Scotland. But with these there has also a Great Number of New Lights and Independants come here from New England, and many Baptists from thence, being driven from, and not able to live there among the Saints —Some of these maintain their Teachers. But to keep up their Interests, and preserve their People from falling off to the Church established, and to keep them in a Knott together, the Synods of Pensylvania and New England send out a Sett of Rambling fellows Yearly—who do no Good to the People, no Service to Religion— but turning of their Brains and picking up their Pockets of ev'ry Pistreen the Poor Wretches have, return back again, with double the Profits I can make—for tho' the Law gives me 12/6 Currency for ev'ry Baptism, I never yet took one farthing—and of near 100 Couple that I've married, I have not been paid for 1/3. Their Poverty is so Great, that were they to offer me a fee, my Heart would not let me take it.

'Tis these roving Teachers that stir up the Minds of the People against the Establish'd Church, and her Ministers—and make the Situation of any Gentleman extremely uneasy, vexatious, and disagreeable. I would sooner starve in England on a Curacy of 20£ p ann, than to live here on 200 Guineas, did not the Interests of Religion and the Church absolutely require it—Some few of these Itinerants have encountered me—I find them a Sett of Rhapsodists— Enthusiasts—Bigots—Pedantic, illiterate, impudent Hypocrites— Straining at Gnats, and swallowing Camels, and making Religion a

Cloak for Covetuousness Detraction, Guile, Impostures and their particular Fabric of Things.

Among these Quakers and Presbyterians, are many concealed Papists—They are not tolerated in this Government—And in the Shape of New Light Preachers, I've met with many Jesuits. We have too here a Society of *Dunkards*—these resort to hear me when I am over at Jacksons Creek.

Among this Medley of Religions—True Genuine Christianity is not to be found. And the perverse persecuting Spirit of the Presbyterians, displays it Self much more here than in Scotland. It is dang'rous to live among, or near any of them—for if they cannot cheat, rob, defraud or injure You in Your Goods—they will belye, defame, lessen, blacken, disparage the most valuable Person breathing, not of their Communion in his Character, Good Name, or Reputation and Credit. They have almost worm'd out all the Church People—who cannot bear to live among such a Sett of Vile unaccountable Wretches.

These Sects are eternally jarring among themselves—The Presbyterians hate the Baptists far more than they do the Episcopalians, and so of the Rest—But (as in England) they will unite altogether —in a Body to distress or injure the Church establish'd.

Hence it is, that when any Bills have been presented to the Legislature to promote the Interests of Religion, these Sectaries have found Means to have them overruled, for the leading Men of the House being all Lawyers, those People know how to grease Wheels to make them turn.

If Numbers were to be counted here, the Church People would have the Majority—But in Point of Interest, I judge that the Dissenters possess most Money—and thereby they can give a Bias to things at Pleasure.

The Grand Juries have presented as a Greivance, the Shame and Damage arising from such Itinerant Teachers being suffer'd to ramble about—They have even married People under my Eye in defiance of all Laws and Regulations—And I can get no Redress—I do all the Duty—take all the Pains. If there is a Shilling to be got by a Wedding or Funeral, these Impudent fellows will endeavour to pocket it: and are the most audacious of any Sett of Mortals I ever met with—They beat any Medicinal Mountebank.

•   •   •

They have now got a Schoolmaster at this Place. An old Presbyterian fellow, or between that and a Quaker—They send their Children to him readily, and pay him, tho' they would not to me, who would have educated them Gratis. Such is their atachment to their Kirk.—Some call me a Jesuit—and the Liturgy the Mass—I have observ'd what Tricks they would have play'd on Christmas Day, to have disturbed the People. I will mention another.

Not long after, they hir'd a Band of rude fellows to come to Service who brought with them 57 Dogs (for I counted them) which in Time of Service they set fighting, and I was obliged to stop—In Time of Sermon they repeated it—and I was oblig'd to desist and dismiss the People. It is in vain to take up or commit these lawless Ruffians—for they have nothing, and the Charge of sending of them to Charlestown, would take me a Years Salary—We are without any Law, or Order—And as all the Magistrates are Presbyterians, I could not get a Warrant—If I got Warrants as the Constables are Presbyterians likewise, I could not get them serv'd—If serv'd, the Guard would let them escape—Both my Self and other Episcopals have made this Experiment—They have granted me Writs thro' fear of being complain'd off, but took Care not to have them serv'd—I took up one fellow for a Riot at a Wedding, and creating disturbance—The people took up two others for entering the House where I was when in Bed—stealing my Gown—putting it on—and then visiting a Woman in Bed, and getting to Bed to her, and making her give out next day, that the Parson came to Bed to her—This was a Scheme laid by the Baptists—and Man and Woman prepared for the Purpose. The People likewise took up some others for calling of me Jesuit, and railing against the Service—The Constable let them all loose—No bringing of them to Justice—I enter'd Informations against some Magistrates for marrying—but cannot get them out of the other Justices Hands till too late to send to Town for a Judges Warrant.

Another Time (in order to disapoint me of a Congregation, and to laugh at the People) they posted a Paper, signifying, That the King having discovered the Popish Designs of Mr. Woodmason and other Romish Priests in disguise, to bring in Popery and Slavery, had sent over Orders to suspend them all, and to order them to be sent over to England, so that there would be no more preaching for the future. This was believed by some of the Poor Ignorants, and kept them at home.

The Quakers have not been silent any more than their Brethren. This Place was laid out as an Asylum for them. But being unsupported from home, they are come to Nothing—They posted a most virulent Libel at the Meeting House—ridiculing the Liturgy particularly the Absolution—Blessing, and Cross in Baptism—calling me by Name an old Canting Parson. . . .

What I could not effect by Force—or Reason—I have done by Sarcasm—for at the Time when they sent the fellows with their Dogs, one of the Dogs followed me down here—which I carried to the House of one of the principals—and told Him that I had 57 Presbyterians came that Day to Service, and that I had converted one of them, and brought Him home—I left the Dog with Him—This Joke has made them so extremely angry that they could cut my Throat— But I've gained my Aim, having had no disturbance from them since —for if a Presbyterian now shews his face at Service, our People ask him if he is come to be *Converted*. So shame has driven them away.

❧

[Stiles]

There are about 15 families of Jews in Newport. Some of the principal of them last year made Application to the Superior Court to be naturalized. The Court declined or defered acting. The Jews then applied to the General Assembly, which refered it to the Superior Court again as their Business to determine, which Superior Court at Newport March Term 1762 gave their Judgment & determination upon the Petition of Aaron Lopez & Isaac Elizur copied [below].

... SUPERIOR COURT, RH. ISL.,
NEWPORT SS. MARCH TERM 1762.

The Petition of Messrs. Aaron Lopez & Isaac Eliezar, Persons professing the Jewish Religion, praying that they may be naturalized on an Act of Parliament made in the 13th year of his Majesty's Reign George the Second, having been duly considered, and also the Act of Parliament therein referred to, the Court are unanimously of Opinion that the said Act of Parliament was wisely designed for increasing the Number of Inhabitants in the Plantations, but this Colony being already so full of people that many of his Majesty's good Subjects born within the same have removed & settled in Nova Scotia & other places, cannot come within the Intention of the said Act. Further by the Charter granted to this Colony it appears that the full & quiet enjoyment of the Christian Religion & a Desire of propagating the same were the principal Views with which the Colony was settled, & by a Law made & past in the year 1663 no person who does not profess the Christian Religion can be admitted free of this Colony; this Court therefore unanimously dismiss the said Petition as abso-

lutely inconsistent with the first Principle upon which the Colony was
founded & a Law of the same in full Force.

. . . The Jews were called up to hear their . . . mortifying sentence and Judgment which dismissed their Petition for Naturalization. . . . Providence seems to make every Thing to work for Mor-
tification to the Jews, & to prevent their incorporating into any Nation;
that thus they may continue a distinct people. Tho' the Naturalization
Act passed the Parliament a few years ago, yet it produced such a national Disgust towards the Hebrews, that the Jews themselves joyned
in Petition to Parliament to repeal that Act, & it was thereupon
repealed, for Britain. And tho' it was continued by way of Permission in the Plantations upon 7 Years' Residence, yet the Tumult at
New York in procuring the Taking place of their Naturalization
there, & the Opposition it has met with in Rh. Island, forbodes that
the Jews will never become incorporated with the people of America,
any more than in Europe, Asia & Africa.

23.—RELIGIOUS INDIFFERENCE

*Some observers of American colonial life noted that a side-
effect of religious variety and toleration was the growth of
religious apathy. Crevecoeur's explanation of how it came
about is the classic account.—From Hector St. John de
Crevecoeur,* Letters from an American Farmer *(New York,
1908), pp. 61-66.*

As I have endeavoured to shew you how Europeans become Americans; it may not be disagreeable to shew you likewise how the various Christian sects introduced, wear out, and how religious indifference becomes prevalent. When any considerable number of a particular sect happen to dwell contiguous to each other, they immediately
erect a temple, and there worship the Divinity agreeably to their own
peculiar ideas. Nobody disturbs them. If any new sect springs up in
Europe, it may happen that many of its professors will come and
settle in America. As they bring their zeal with them, they are at
liberty to make proselytes if they can, and to build a meeting and to
follow the dictates of their consciences; for neither the government
nor any other power interferes. If they are peaceable subjects, and

are industrious, what is it to their neighbours how and in what manner they think fit to address their prayers to the Supreme Being? But if the sectaries are not settled close together, if they are mixed with other denominations, their zeal will cool for want of fuel, and will be extinguished in a little time. Then the Americans become as to religion, what they are as to country, allied to all. In them the name of Englishman, Frenchman, and European is lost, and in like manner, the strict modes of Christianity as practised in Europe are lost also. . . . Let the following example serve as my first justification.

Let us suppose you and I to be travelling; we observe that in this house, to the right, lives a Catholic, who prays to God as he has been taught, and believes in transubstantion; he works and raises wheat, he has a large family of children, all hale and robust; his belief, his prayers offend nobody. About one mile farther on the same road, his next neighbour may be a good honest plodding German Lutheran, who addresses himself to the same God, the God of all, agreeably to the modes he has been educated in, and believes in consubstantiation; by so doing he scandalizes nobody; he also works in his fields, embellishes the earth, clears swamps, &c. What has the world to do with his Lutheran principles? He persecutes nobody, and nobody persecutes him, he visits his neighbours, and his neighbours visit him. Next to him lives a seceder, the most enthusiastic of all sectaries; his zeal is hot and fiery, but separated as he is from others of the same complexion, he has no congregation of his own to resort to, where he might cabal and mingle religious pride with worldly obstinacy. He likewise raises good crops, his house is handsomely painted, his orchard is one of the fairest in the neighbourhood. How does it concern the welfare of the country, or of the province at large, what this man's religious sentiments are, or really whether he has any at all? He is a good farmer, he is a sober, peaceable, good citizen: William Penn himself would not wish for more. This is the visible character, the invisible one is only guessed at, and is nobody's business. Next again lives a Low Dutchman, who implicitly believes the rules laid down by the synod of Dort. He conceives no other idea of a clergyman than that of an hired man; if he does his work well he will pay him the stipulated sum; if not he will dismiss him, and do without his sermons, and let his church be shut up for years. But notwithstanding this coarse idea, you will find his house and farm to be the neatest in all the country; and you will judge by his waggon and fat horses, that he thinks more of the affairs of this world than of those of the next. He is sober and laborious, therefore he is all he ought to be as to the affairs of this life; as for those of the next, he must trust to the great Creator. Each of these people instruct their children as well as they can, but these instructions are feeble compared to those which are given to the youth of the poorest class in Europe. Their children will therefore grow up less zealous and more indifferent in matters of religion than their parents. The foolish vanity, or rather the fury of making Proselytes, is unknown here; they have no time, the seasons call for all their attention, and thus in a few years, this mixed neighbourhood will exhibit a strange religious medley, that will be neither pure Catholicism nor pure Calvinism. A very perceptible indifference even in the first generation, will become apparent; and it may happen that the daughter of the Catholic will marry the son of the seceder, and settle by themselves at a distance from their parents. What religious education will they give their children? A very imperfect one. If there happens to be in the neighbourhood any place of worship, we will suppose a Quaker's meeting; rather than not shew their fine clothes, they will go to it, and some of them may perhaps attach themselves to that society. Others will remain in a perfect state of indifference; the children of these zealous parents will not be able to tell what their religious principles are, and their grandchildren still less. The neighbourhood of a place of worship generally leads them to it, and the action of going thither, is the strongest evidence they can give of their attachment to any sect. The Quakers are the only people who retain a fondness for their own mode of worship; for be they ever so far separated from each other, they hold a sort of communion with the society, and seldom depart from its rules, at least in this country. Thus all sects are mixed as well as all nations; thus religious indifference is imperceptibly disseminated from one end of the continent to the other; which is at present one of the strongest characteristics of the Americans. . . .

24.—RELIGIOUS ENTHUSIASM

While some colonists succumbed to religious indifference, others took part in America's first great religious revival. From the 1720s to the 1760s, almost any evangelical preacher drew huge audiences. But the master spellbinder throughout the period was the English missionary George

*Whitefield, who made seven visits to the American colonies
between 1738 and 1770. Nathan Cole of Kensington, Connecticut, recorded his own reaction to Whitefield's presence.
—Quoted in George L. Walker,* Some Aspects of the Religious Life of New England . . . (*New York, 1897*), *pp.
89-91.*

Now it pleased god to send mr. whitfeld into this land & my hearing of his preaching at philadelphia like one of the old aposels, &
many thousands floocking after him to hear the gospel and great numbers were converted to Christ, i felt the spirit of god drawing me by
conviction i longed to see & hear him & wished he would come this
way and i soon heard he was come to new york & the jases [Jerseys]
& great multitudes flocking after him under great concern for their
Soule & many converted wich brought on my concern more & more
hoping soon to see him but next i herd he was on long iland & next
at boston & next at northampton & then one morning all on a Suding
about 8 or 9 o Clock there came a messenger & said mr. whitfeld
preached at hartford & weathersfield yesterday & is to preach at
middeltown this morning [October 23, 1740] at 10 o clock i was in
my field at work i dropt my tool that i had in my hand & run home
& run throu my house & bad my wife get ready quick to goo and hear
mr. whitfeld preach at middeltown & run to my pasture for my hors
with all my might fearing i should be too late to hear him i brought
my hors home & soon mounted & took my wife up & went forward
as fast as i thought the hors could bear, & when my hors began to
be out of breath i would get down & put my wife on the Saddel &
bid her ride as fast as she could & not Stop or Slak for me except
i bad her & so i would run untill i was almost out of breth & then
mount my hors again & so i did severel times to favour my hors we
improved every moment to get along as if we was fleeing for our
lives all this while fearing we should be too late to hear the Sarmon
for we had twelve miles to ride dubble in littel more then an hour &
we went round by the upper housen parish & when we came within
about half a mile of the road that comes down from hartford weathersfield & stepney to middeltown on high land i saw before me a Cloud
or fog rising i first thought off from the great river but as i came
nearer the road i heard a noise something like a low rumbling thunder & i presently found it was the rumbling of horses feet coming
down the road & this Cloud was a Cloud of dust made by the running of horses feet it arose some rods into the air over the tops of
the hills & trees & when i came within about twenty rods of the road

i could see men & horses Sliping along in the Cloud like shadows &
when i came nearer it was like a stedy streem of horses & their riders
scarcely a horse more then his length behind another all of a lather
and fome with swet ther breath rooling out of their noistrels in the
cloud of dust every jump every hors semed to go with all his might
to carry his rider to hear the news from heaven for the saving of
their Souls it made me trembel to see the Sight how the world was
in a strugle i found a vacance between two horses to Slip in my hors
& my wife said law our cloaths will be all spoiled see how they look
for they was so covered with dust that thay looked allmost all of a
coler coats & hats & shirts & horses We went down in the Streem
i herd no man speak a word all the way three mile but evry one
presing forward in great hast & when we gat down to the old meating
house thare was a great multitude it was said to be 3 or 4000 of
people asembled together we gat of from our horses & shook off the
dust and the ministers was then coming to the meating house i turned
and looked toward the great river & saw the fery boats running swift
forward & backward bringing over loads of people the ores roed
nimble & quick every thing men horses & boats all seamed to be
struglin for life the land & the banks over the river lookt black with
people & horses all along the 12 miles i see no man at work in his
field but all seamed to be gone—when i see mr. whitfeld come up
upon the Scaffil he looked almost angellical a young slim slender
youth before some thousands of people & with a bold undainted countenance & my hearing how god was with him every where as he came
along it solumnized my mind & put me in a trembling fear before he
began to preach for he looked as if he was Cloathed with authority
from the great god, & a sweet sollome Solemnity sat upon his brow
& my hearing him preach gave me a heart wound by gods blessing
my old foundation was broken up & i saw that my righteousness
would not save me. . . .

VI

Colonial Modes
of Government and Law

Most aspects of the political and legal systems of Colonial America were patterned after England's. Most colonial governments had royal governors, appointed councils, and elected lower houses. Most also had systems of superior and inferior courts which administered justice in accordance with age-old British traditions.

But the transfer of political and judicial ideas from the mother country to the colonies was never complete, and as the provincial period wore on the gap between England's example and America's practice became increasingly obvious. Newcomers and foreign visitors quickly noted the greater percentage of voters (thanks to the ease of meeting the property qualification), the decreasing influence of royal authority, the growing participation of ordinary citizens in local government, the diminishing reliance on common law, the absence (until late in the eighteenth century) of a skilled legal profession, and the emergence of less traditional procedures of jurisprudence. These and other characteristics gave an increasing American cast to the administration of the colonies.

At the same time, the colonies displayed a confusing variety of political systems, as each province evolved its own blend of English antecedent and American preference. Most of the colonies can be classified as royal because their governors and councilors received appointments from the Crown, yet two colonies (Maryland and Pennsylvania) were semi-feudal possessions of hereditary proprietors, and two others (Connecticut and Rhode Island) enjoyed almost complete self-government under corporate charters. And even within these general categories—royal, proprietary, and corporate—the central ad-

ministration of each colony differed in significant ways from those of
its neighbors. By the same token, the colonies had a wide variety of
local political institutions—New England favoring the town-meeting
system with its profusion of popularly elected servants, and most of
the southern colonies showing preference for county officials appointed by the governor: sheriffs, justices of the peace, constables,
and the like.

In every colony, however, the number of people actively involved
in the process of government and the administration of justice was
remarkably higher than in England or on the Continent. In royal
colonies as well as in corporate and proprietary colonies, voters
made frequent and often vehement use of their franchise. They also
took eager advantage of their courts of law to resolve the inter-
minable disputes which were an unavoidable aspect of their burgeon-
ing society. More than one visitor noted that Americans seemed to
thrive on litigation.

25.—TOWN-MEETING DEMOCRACY

*Nowhere in Colonial America were the people more di-
rectly involved in the political process than in the New
England colonies. There the inhabitants of each town gathered periodically to resolve a multitude of local issues and
to elect town officials. Below are glimpses of several town
meetings held during the 1720s in Plymouth, Massachusetts,
as witnessed by the Town Recorder.—From* Records of the
Town of Plymouth, II, 1705 to 1743 *(Plymouth, Mass.,
1892), 230-233, 237-239, 243-249, 251-252, 254-255, 257, 266,
268-271.*

At a Town meeting held at Plymouth in the Court House on the
fifteenth day of february 1725 The Grand Jurors Chosen for the
year are Stephen Churchell Ephraim Kempton & Joseph Mitchell
The Jurors Chosen to serve at the Quarter Sessions on the first
tuesday of March next are Capt Samuel Drew John Cooke & Robert
Finney

John Watson Esq was chosen an agent to answer the Towns pre-
sentment at the next quarter Sessions At said Meeting there was a
long debate about a School or Schools and after some time there

was a voate called whether they would have three schools & there
being a great assembly it was something difficult to distinguish the
voate by holding up the hand and it was thereupon ordered by the
Moderator that the assembly should withdraw out of the House &
then to Come in & pass by the Clark & declare whether they were
for one or three schools and it was voated by a Majority of voates
that there should be one school. And there being a great tumult in
the meeting and the people difficult to be settled the Moderator therefore adjorned the present meeting to the first day of March next to
meet at ten o clock in the forenoon at the usual place of meeting

At a Town meeting held at Plymouth on the first day of March
1725 at the Court House In Plymouth for the Choice of Town officers and Regulateing & fixing the School The Town proceeded to
the Choice of Town officers. Mr. Josiah Cotton Esq chosen Moderator John Dyer chosen Town Clerk & sworn by Josiah Cotton Esq
The Selectmen are Isaac Lothrop Esq Decon John Foster John Dyer
Jacob Mitchell & Josiah Morton

Voated that there be five Assessors, and the Assessors Chosen are
Isaac Lothrop Esq John Dyer Decon John Foster Jacob Mitchell &
Josiah Morton.

Voated that there be four Constables. The Constables Chosen are
William Bradford Senior Nathaniel Thomas Thomas Bartlett and
Samuel Baites. And the said Nathaniel Thomas refused to serve and
he paid five pounds. And the Town then proceeded on another
choice & Choose Samuel Bartlett and there being two Samuel Bartlets in the Town it was uncertain which of said Bartlets should serve
by reason many of the voters declared they Intended Samuel Bartlett
Junior. Therefore voated that Samuel Bartlett formerly of Dux-
berough now in Plymouth should be Excused from serving as Constable this present year. And the Town proceeded again to another
Choice & Choose Samuel Bartlett Junior to serve as Constable.

John Dyer was Chosen to be Town Treasurer for the year Ensuing.

Josiah Morton Thomas Holmes & William Cooke Chosen Surveyors of the Highways

Voated that the Selectmen of the Town agree with the Surveyors
to mend the Highways within the Town for the term of seven years
from this day and that they be paid annually out of The Town
Treasury the sum of twelve pence per Head for every Ratable Poll

and that the Selectmen take proper Bonds of them concerning the said affair so as to Indemnify the Town. Bridges to be mended according to Late Agreements.

And then the Town proceeded to manage the affair about the school

Voated that the Grammer School (in which also is to be taught Writing Reading & Arethmetick as usual) be kept in the middle of the Town near the Meeting House or Court House from the Twentieth of April next for the space of seven years next coming

Voated that John Watson Esq John Dyer & Mr Haviland Torry be a Commite to provide a suitable Schoolmaster from time to time dureing said space.

And also at the same time Voated that each end of the Town who for some years past had a Womans School among them be allowed to deduct out of the Town Treasury what they are annually voted or taxed for the Grammer Schoole and no more towards the maintaining a School among themselves. Provided they see cause to keep one.

• • •

At an adjornment of the Town meeting from the first day of March 1725 to the 29th of March Instant the Inhabitants of said Town met at the usual place of meeting: At said meeting Thomas Bartlett appeared and made a plea that he ought not to serve in the place of a Constable this present yeare by Reason that he was at half the Charge in hireing a man to go in the service to the Eastward Last Summer. And the Town voated that the said Thomas Bartlett be Excused to serve in the office of a Constable this present year. And the Town Proceeded to another choice of a Constable and the Town made choice of Robert Finney to serve in the office of Constable for the Ensuing year

The Tythingmen Chosen are Samuell Cornish William Bradford Junior Eleazer Morton Thomas Spooner & Joshua Gibs

The Fence viewers Chosen are Thomas Holmes John Barnes Ebenezar Holmes Thomas Clarke Decons Son and Robert Cushman. And the said Persons are Chosen to be feild drivers

Voated that the swine be kept up this present year Voated that the North part of the Town so far as to Include Mr. John Sturtevant & Josiah Cotton Esq have Liberty to Let their swine run at Large under the regulation of the Law.

The Hog Reves Chosen are Benjamin Rider Joseph Bartlett Samuel Marshall Elkanah Churchell Jonathan Bryant Inholder Jacob Mitchell Elisha Stetson James Warren and Joseph Warren

The Jurors Chosen for the Superior Court to be holden at Plymouth on the Last tuesday of April next. The Grand Jurors Chosen are John Dyer & Mr John Barnes to serve at said Court

The Persons Chosen to serve on the Jury of Tryals at said Court are Mr Thomas Morton Decon John Wood Mr Jacob Mitchell & Mr Josiah Morton.

At a Town Meeting held at Plymouth in the Court House on the 9th day of August 1725 . . .

* * *

At said meeting it was moved whether the Inhabitants of the South part of this Town at Ele River and Manument Ponds should have a Reading and writing School among them to be maintained by the Town as it was the last year and some years before to be kept for the space of seven years from the 20th of April last and the money to be drawn yearly out of the Town Treasurie for said seven years or so long a time as they keep school within the said seven years Provided that it does not Exceed 20£ a year with what they are to draw of their Rates by the voat of the 1st of March Last past. Voated in the Negative Voated That Capt Benjamin Warren and Mr Josiah Morton be a Committe to provide a school at Ele River and Manument Ponds from time to time and to draw out of the Town Treasurie what the said part of the Town pay by way of Rate towards the Grammar School according to the vote of the first of March Last past.

* * *

Pursuant to the voate at a Town meeting held at Plymouth on the 2d day of March 1711 For and and (c.q.) in Consideration of the sum of Thirty and five shillings by Thomas Wetherell of said Plymouth unto John Dyer Town Treasurer of said Plymouth well and truely paid for the use of the said Town. The Town hath Given Granted bargained made over and Confirmed unto him the said Thomas Wetherell & unto his heires & assignes for Ever a certain peice of Land Lying being & bounded as followeth. Plymouth March 26th 1725. Layd out by us the subscribers unto Thomas Wetherell and is bounded as followeth viz: Beginning at the North End of Docter Lebarons stable near the meeting House to the Norward of said stable to Extend Thirty feet in the front and Twenty feet Back into the hill Leaving Eighteen feet in Wedth Between Mr John Murdocks Barn & the said Lott, with the priviledge for said Wetherell To heave out his Dung on the southerly or upper side of said Lott, Valued at Thirty five shillings.

Isaac Lothrop⎫ Surveyers
Benjamin Warren⎭ & aprizers

At an adjornment of the Town meeting from the Seventh day of March 1726 to the tenth day of March Instant

• • •

. . . There was a Voate called whether the swine should run at Large this year under the Regulation of the Law and it passed in the Negative

Notwithstanding the voate that is already made about swine as abovesaid upon a motion made by several of the Inhabitants of the Ends of the Town. Voated that the swine shall run at Large all within the North Precinct and so far on the south side of the Town as Ele River, under the Regulation of the Law.

• • •

. . . There being a motion made about Encorigment of Killing black birds & Crows. Voted that something be paid to such persons as should Kill any black birds or Crows within the Town of Plymouth. Voated that what Black birds or Crows shall be Killed by any Persons within the Town of Plymouth they shall be paid out of the Town Treasury the sum of Two pence per head for black birds & the sum of four pence per head for Crows that shall be Killed from the first day of March to the Last day of June next. Voated that they bring what black birds & Crows they shall Kill within said Term and deliver them to the Town Treasurer on the Last day of May next and on the Last day of June following for which the Town Treasurer shall pay them as abovesaid out of the Town Treasurie They first giveing good satisfaction to the Treasur that such black birds & Crows were killed within the Town of Plymouth.

At a Town meeting held at Plymouth by the Inhabitants of Plymouth and that part of Kingston which Lately did belong to Plymouth on the 5th day of September 1726.

• • •

An accompt of what is necessary to be raised on the Inhabitants

abovesaid both on Poles and Estates was presented to the Town which
is as followeth

To the Representative......................[£]	25.00.00
To the Assessors...........................	6.00.00
To the poor................................	20.00.00
To the s[c]hool	30.00.00
To Ele River Bridge........................	6.00.00
To the Treasurers Commissions..............	7.13.00
To the surveyers about the highways........	20.00.00
To the Town Bridg & other uses.............	15.07.00

[£] 130.00.00

Voated that the said sum of [£]130.00.00 should be raised on the
Inhabitants of Plymouth & that part of Kingston which Lately did
belong to Plymouth both upon Poles & Estates.

At the Town Meeting Last mentioned by the Inhabitants of Plymouth onely there was an accompt presented of what was necessary
to be raised for the Ministers Salery & Saxton &c which is as
followeth

To the Ministers Salery....................[£]	110.00.00
To the Assessors...........................	2.00.00
To the meeting house glass & other repairs...	16.00.00
To the Saxton.............................	10.00.00
To the Treasurers Commissions.............	3.04.00

[£] 141.04.00

Voated that the said sum of [£]141.04.00 should be raised on the
Inhabitants of Plymouth both on Poles & Estates to defrey the above
said Charge

Voated that the Inhabitants of Plymouth pay their Ministers Rate
by Contribution if they see cause and that they mark their money
and all that is unmarked shall be accounted strangers money which
the Reverend Mr Nathaniel Leonard shall have the benefit off [of]
and the said Reverend Mr Nathaniel Leonard be desired to keep an
accompt of each mans money that is so marked.

Voated that the Representatives wages be raised for this present
year both for the time past and yet to come of said year. Voated
that there be one shilling per day be paid to Decon John Foster our
present Representative for so many days as he hath or shall attend
the service of the Great & General Court which is one shilling more
than what the Law at present allows, & so make it five shillings per
day dureing this present year.

At a Legall Town Meeting held at Plymouth on the 13th day of March 1727

•   •   •

Voated that there be Encorigment given to those persons that shall kill any wild cats within the Township of Plymouth to be paid out of the Town Treasury. Voated that there shall be ten shillings paid out of the Town Treasury per head to every of the Inhabitants of the Town of Plymouth that shall kill any wild cats within the limits of said Town they produceing and order from the persons hereafter named Voated that John Watson Esq & Mr John Murdock shall receive the heads of the wild cats that shall be Killed within said Town and give orders to the Town Treasurer for the payment of them.

At a Town Meeting held at Plymouth in the Court House on the 15th of May 1727 . . .

•   •   •

Voted that the Selectmen of this Town with Mr Watson Mr Murdock Mr John Barnes & Mr Stephen Churchell be a Committe to find & Provide a Convenient Place upon the Common to set the Gallows upon for the Execution of the Condemned Prisoner.

At a Town Meeting held at Plymouth in the Court House August 28th 1727

•   •   •

Voated that there be several places in Town appointed for to set up notifications of any Cattle or sheep straying about their Houses or Inclosures from the first of September next to the latter end of December following so annually from year to year And that at Eell River at the House of Capt Benjamin Warrens be one place and at Town at the House of Mr Thomas Wetherell be another place and at the House of Mr Thomas Holmes be the third place and all Persons are desired to Conforme to the above said vote and as stray Cattle & Sheep shall frequent about their Dwellings To sett up their Notis with Naturall & Artificiall marks so that the owners of said Cattle may come by an easier way to know where they are and make satisfaction accordingly

At a Town Meeting held at Plymouth on the 13th day of November 1727

. . .

Voated that there be an Alms House built for the Entertainment of the Poor of the Town of Plymouth

Voated that John Watson Esq Mr John Murdock & Mr Josiah Carver be a Committe to take care to provide Materials for to build said House. And also voted that the said Committe advise with the Selectmen about the building of said House

Voted that Eleaser Donham shall have fourty shillings paid him out of the Town Treasury to get him a great coat.

At a Town Meeting held at Plymouth in the Court House on the 25th day of December 1727

. . .

Voated that there be a Committe to prevent the Wasting & destroying of the fish called alewives the Committe are Decon John Foster Stephen Churchell Decon Haviland Torry Timothy Morton and Thomas Spooner. Voted that none of the Inhabitants of the Town of Plymouth whatsoever shall take any of said fish either with nets or saines nor by beating of them in the Town Brooke or any where in the harbour of Plymouth and to put them into or any other cask & Expose them to sale Excepting what they may have occation for to use themselves for baite & their families use.

Voted that no stranger whatsoever that comes into the Town of Plymouth shall take any of the alewives either with a net or saine or by beating of them in the Town Brooke or any where in the Harbour of Plymouth without licence first obtained from the Committe and if they shall proceed contrary to this Act the said Committe are fully Impowered to prosecute him or them that shall transgress therein

At a Town Meeting held at Plymouth on the 29th day of January 1730 . . .

. . .

Voated that there be the sum of fifty pounds raised to help to support the Charges of our Ajency in England in the defence of our priviledges.

At an Adjornment of the Town Meeting from the 16th day of March to the last Munday of March Instant 1730.

•   •   •

Voted that there be a Committe to Examine adjust & proportion the charge of the several accompts of the sundrey persons that have been lately sick of the Small pox. The persons chosen for said Committee are Nathaniel Thomas Esq Isaac Lathrop Esq & John Dyer. Voted that Mr John Murdock John Dyer & Stephen Churchell James Warren & Joseph Bartlett be a Committee to take care to regulate affairs about preventing the Infection of the Small poxs spreading. . . .

Voted that the Town Treasurer be Impowred to prosecute any person or persons that are Indebted to the Town for what charge the said Town was at either for Nursing tendance or other Necessaries in the time of the Small pox.

At a Town Meeting held at Plymouth in the Court House on the 11th day of May 1730

•   •   •

At said Meeting the Town made choice of Mr Nathaniel Jackson & Samuel Kempton to be added to the Committe which are to take care about the vessels and persons that come from & go to Boston and what goods they bring from thence that may be thought to be Infected with the small pox to do what may be suposed to be propper to prevent the Inhabitants being infected therewith.

At a Town Meeting held at Plymouth on the fifteenth day of June 1730 The Town . . .

•   •   •

Voted that the Town Treasurer be Impowred to gather in the money that is due to the Town of Plymouth from the several persons that have been lately sick with the Small pox for what was Expended on them for nurses & necessaries as appears by their Several Bills. And to prosecute any person or persons that shall neglect or refuse to make payment of their several Bills.

At a Town Meeting held at Plymouth on the fourteenth day of September 1730 . . .

•   •   •

Voted that the affair about the Alewives & unruly Dogs be continued to next Town Meeting. Voted that the affair about the Sedge in the Town Pond be continued to the next Town Meeting. Voted that the Constables (viz) David Turner & Thomas Faunce the Elders son shall take care that the children & youths in the Town of Plymouth may be well regulated on the Lords day till the next Town Meeting.

26.—DEMOCRACY AND DEFERENCE IN NEW YORK

The enthusiasm with which the people sometimes exercised the political franchise, and their tendency to use it in favor of the local aristocracy, are reflected in this excerpt from the New York Weekly Journal *of November 5, 1733, reporting an election of the previous week.—From a copy at The New-York Historical Society.*

Westchester, October 29th, 1733.

On this Day, *Lewis Morris,* Esq., late Chief Justice of this Province, was by a great Majority of Voices, elected a Representative for the County of *Westchester.*

This being an Election of great Expectation, and where in the Court and Country's Interest was exerted (as is said) to the Utmost: I shall give my Readers, a particular Account of it, as I had it from a Person that was present at it.

Nicholas Cooper, Esq., High Sheriff of the said County, having by Papers affixed to the Church of *East-Chester,* and other Publick Places, given Notice of the Day and Place of Election, without mentioning any Time of the Day, when it was to be done; which made the Electors on the Side of the late Judge, verry Suspitious that some Fraud was intended: To prevent which about 50 of them kept Watch upon and about, the Green at *Eastchester,* (the Place of Election,) from 12 o'Clock the Night before, 'til the Morning of that Day: The other Electors begining to move on Sunday Afternoon and Evening, so as to be at *New-Rochell,* by Midnight, their Way lay through

Harrison's Purchase, the Inhabitants of which provided for their
Entertainment, as they pass'd each House in their Way, having a
Table plentifully covered for that Purpose; about Midnight they all
met at the House of *William Lecount,* at *New-Rochell,* whose House
not being large enough to entertain so great a Number, a large Fire
was made in the Street, by which they sat 'til Day-Light, at which
Time they began to move; they were joynd on the Hill at the East
end of the Town, by about 70 Horse of the Electors of the lower
Part of the County, and then proceeded towards the Place of Election in the following Order, *viz.* First rode two Trumpeters and 3
Violines; next 4 of the principal Freeholders, one of which carried a
Banner, on one Side of which was affixed in gold Capitals, KING
GEORGE, and on the Other, in like golden Capitals LIBERTY & LAW;
next followed the Candidate *Lewis Morris* Esq., late Chief Justice
of this Province; then two Colours; and at Sun rising they entered
upon the Green of *Eastchester* the Place of Election, follow'd by
above 300 Horse of the principal Freeholders of the County, (a
greater Number than had ever appear'd for one Man since the Settlement of that County:) After having rode three Times round the
Green, they went to the Houses of *Joseph Fowler* and —— *Child,*
who were well prepared for their Reception, and the late Chief Justice, on his allighting by several Gentleman, who came there to give
their Votes for him.

About Eleven of the Clock appeared the Candidate of the other
Side, *William Forster* Esq., School Master, appointed by the Society
for Propagation of the Gospel, and lately made by Commission from
his Excellency (the present Governour,) Clerk of the Peace and
common Pleas, in that County; which Commission it is said, he purchased for the valuable Consideration of One Hundred Pistoles given
the Governor; next him, came two Ensignes, born by two of the
Freeholders; then followed the Honourable *James Delaney,* Esq.,
Chief Justice of the Province of *New-York,* and the Honourable
Fredrick Philipse, Esq., second Judge of the said Province, and
Baron of the EXCHEQUER, attended by about 170 Horse of the
Freeholders and Friends of the said *Forster;* and the two Judges
they entred the Green on the *East* side, and riding twice round it,
their Word was *No Land-Tax,* as they passed, the second Judge very
civilly saluted the late Chief Justice by taking off his Hat, which the
late Judge returned in the same Manner: Some of the late Judges
Party crying out no *Excise,* and one of them was heard to say (tho
not by the Judge) no Pretender, upon which, *Forster,* the Candidate,
reply'd, *I will take Notice of you,* they after that, retired to the House

of ——— *Baker,* which was prepared to recieve and entertain them. About an Hour after, the High Sheriff came to Town finely mounted, the Housings and Holster-Caps being Scarlet, richly laced with Silver belonging to ———: Upon his approach the Electors on both Sides went into the Green, where they were to Elect, and after having read his Majesty's Writ, bid the Electors proceed to the Choice which they did; and a great Majority appeard for Mr. *Morris,* the late Judge: Upon which a Poll was demanded, but by whom is not known to the Relator, tho' it was said by many, to be done by the Sheriff himself. *Morris,* the Candidate several Times asked the Sheriff upon whose Side the Majority appeard, but could get no other reply, but that a Poll must be had, and accordingly after about two Hours delay, in geting Benches, Chairs, and Tables they began to Poll: Soon after one of those called Quakers, a Man of known Worth and Estate, came to give his Vote for the late Judge, upon this *Forster* and the two *Fowlers, Moses* and *William,* chosen by him to be Inspectors questioned his having an Estate, and required of the Sheriff to tender him the Book to Swear, in due Form of Law, which he refused to do, but offered to take his solemn Affirmation; which noth by the Laws of *England* and the Laws of this Province was indulged to the People called Quakers, and had always been practised from the first Election of Representatives, in this Province to this Time, and never refused; but the Sheriff was deaf to all that could be alledged on that Side; and notwithstanding, that he was told both by the late Chief Justice, and *James Alexander,* Esq; One of His Majesty's Council, and Councellor at Law, and by *William Smith,* Esq; Councellor at Law, That such a Procedure was contrary to Law, and a violent Attempt of the Liberties of the People: He still presisted in refusing the said Quaker to Vote; and in like Manner did refuse Seven and Thirty Quakers more, Men of known and visible Estates.

This *Cooper,* now High-Sheriff of the said County, is said, not only to be a Stranger in that County, not having a Foot of Land, or other visible Estate in it, unless very lately granted; and it is believ'd, he has not where with all to purchase any.

The Polling had not been long continued, before Mr. *Edward Stephens,* a Man of a very considerable Estate in the said County, did openly in the Hearing of all the Freeholders there assembled, charge *William Forster,* Esq; the Candidate on the other Side, with being a *Jacobite,* and in the Interest of the *Pretender;* and that he should say to Mr. *William Willet,* (a Person of good Estate, and known Integrity, who was at that Time present, and ready to make Oath to the Truth of what was said) that true it was, he had taken

the Oaths to his Majesty King GEORGE, and enjoy'd a Place in
the Government under Him, which gave him Bread: Yet notwithstanding That, should—*James* come into *England,* he should think
himself oblig'd to go there and Fight for him. This was loudly and
strongly urged to *Forster's* Face, who denied it to be true; and no
more was said of it at that Time.

About Eleven o'Clock that Night the Poll was clos'd. And it stood
thus:

> For the late Chief Justice,.......... 231
> Quakers,........................ 38
> ————
> In all............................ 269
> ════
> For *William Forster*, Esq;.......... 151
> The Difference.................... 118
> ————
> 269

So that the late Chief Justice carried it by a great Majority, without
the Quakers. Upon closing the Poll, the other Candidate, *Forster,*
and the Sheriff, wish'd the late Chief Justice much Joy. *Forster,*
said, he hop'd the late Judge would not think the worse of him for
setting up against him, to which the Judge reply'd, he *believed that
he was put upon it against his Inclination; but that he was highly
blamable, and who did or should know better for putting the Sheriff,
who was a Stranger and ignorant in such Matters, upon making so
violent an Attempt upon the Liberty of the People; which, would
expose him to Ruin, if he were worth £10,000 if the People agriev'd
should commence Suit against him.* The People made a loud Huzza,
which the late Chief Judge blam'd very much, as what he tho't not
right: *Forster* reply'd, *He took no Notice of what the common People
did, since Mr. Morris did not put them upon the doing of it.*

The Indentures being seal'd, the whole Body of Electors, waited
on their new Representative to his Lod[g]ings, with Trumpets sounding, and Violins playing; and in a little Time took their Leave of him:
And thus ended the *Westchester* Election, to the general Satisfaction.

27.—AN ELEMENT OF MONARCHY

Eight of the thirteen colonies that later rebelled against Great Britain were headed by royal governors who represented the authority and dignity of the Crown. Both aspects were reflected in the reception of a new governor, as shown by the following account of Governor Jonathan Belcher's arrival in Massachusetts.—From The Weekly News-Letter *(Boston), August 6-13, 1730.*

Boston, New-England

On Saturday last the 8th Instant [August], about the middle of the Afternoon we were notified by a Signal from Castle *William,* of the near Approach of His Excellency Governor *BELCHER,* in His Majesties Ship of War, the *Blandford,* (Stationed for this Place, Capt. *Prothero* Commander,) appointed for his Transportation; which could reach no further that Night than the Mouth or Entrance of the *Narrows.* Here His Excellency was waited upon, as soon as possible, by an honourable Committee from the General Assembly, with a number of other Gentlemen, who were all received and entertained with that Nobleness and Affability which is natural to the Governeur. The usual Services of the Sabbath were attended by His Excellency at the Castle, with decent and religious Solemnity.

At the opening of the following Day, was the Town of *Boston* in a voluntary Alarm, preparing for His Excellency's Reception & Entertainment. The Troop and Militia were collected, and ranged in the Street below the Town-House, in martial Order, to welcome their Captain-General. The Turrets & Balconies were hung with Carpets, and almost every Vessel was blazon'd with a rich variety of Colours.

Between the Hours of Ten & Eleven His Excellency was pleased to embark for the place of his wonted Residence, with a great Number of Boats & Pinnaces to attend him, while His Majesties Cannon were playing, to inform the Town of his Approach.

At length the Great Object of our Hopes, and reverent Affection, was received & congratulated at the End of the Long-Wharffe, by the Honourable Lieut. Governour & Council, the Judges and Justices, and

an almost numberless Multitude of Gentlemen Spectators. Several
Standards & Ensigns were erected on the Top of Fort-Hill, and at
Clark's Wharffe at the North part of the Town, and a number of
Cannon planted; which were all handsomely Discharged at the arrival
of His Excellency, and followed with such Huzza's as inspired the
whole Town; The Bells all ringing on the joyful Occasion.

While the Pomp was making its orderly Procession, the Guns,
which were bursting in every part of the Town were answered in
mild and rumbling Peals by the Artillery of Heaven, which introduced
the plentiful and refreshing Showers that succeeded a very dry
Season.

After His Majesties Commission was opened and exhibited in the
Council Chamber, and the usual Ceremonies were concluded, the vast
Multitude of Spectators without, express'd, in their united Shouts,
and unusual Joy & Elevation of Soul. The Troops and Regiment
discharged their Duty in triple Vollies; and again were the Cannon
roaring at the Batteries in every part of this Town, and at *Charlestown,* by which the Country was acquainted with the joyful Proclamation.

From the Court-House, His Excellency was conducted by his Civil
& Military Attendants, to a splendid Entertainment at the *Bunch of
Grapes,* & after Dinner to his own pleasant Seat.

The Afternoon was spent in firing, and other Expressions of Joy;
and the Evening concluded with a Bonfire and Illuminations.

By His Excellency

JONATHAN BELCHER, Esq;

Captain General and GOVERNOUR in Chief

in and over His Majesty's Province

of the *Massachusetts-Bay* in *New England,*

and Vice Admiral of the same.

A PROCLAMATION

*His Majesty's Royal Commission constituting & appointing Me to
be Captain General and Governour in Chief of His Majesty's Province of the* Massachusetts-Bay *in* New-England *in* America, *having
on the Day of the Date hereof been Read & Published within the said
Province:*

*I Do therefore by and with the Advice of His Majesty's Council De-
clare and Publish, That all Officers Civil and Military within the
said Province be and hereby are Continued in their respective Of-*

fices, Trusts and Employments, and are Directed and Required to Use and Exercise all and singular the Powers & Authorities to their several & respective Offices belonging, until further Order: Of which all Persons are Commanded to take Notice & Conform themselves Accordingly.

Given at the Council Chamber in *Boston* the Tenth Day of August 1730. In the Fourth Year of the Reign of Our Sovereign Lord GEORGE the Second, by Grace of GOD, of *Great Britain, France* and *Ireland,* KING, Defender of the Faith, etc.

J. BELCHER

By Command of His Excellency, with the Advice of the Council,
Josiah Willard, Secr.

GOD Save the KING.

28.—POLITICAL FRICTION:
COLONY VERSUS CROWN

A new royal governor's glory often did not outlast his reception. He invariably found it impossible both to follow his instructions and at the same time to accommodate the demands of the colonial legislature; the resulting clash could bring government to a standstill. The following letter from Governor George Clinton of New York to the Board of Trade at London reveals how a typical conflict of royal prerogative and representative assembly looked from a governor's chair.—From E. B. O'Callaghan, ed., Documents Relative to the Colonial History of the State of New-York; . . . *(Albany, 1855), VI 57-58.*

My Lords,
I have in my former letters inform'd Your Lordships what Incroachments the Assemblys of this Province have from time to time made on His Majesty's Prerogative & Authority in this Province in drawing an absolute dependence of all the Officers upon them for their Saleries & Reward of their services, & by their taking in effect the Nomination to all Officers, as will appear from former acts, which

I formerly mentioned, and by two Acts the printed copies of which I send Your Lordships, and one Entitled "An Act to make Provision for several services &c and an Act for the payment of the salaries, services & contingencies therein mentioned &c"

That Your Lordships may the better comprehend the Methods which the Assembly have taken to draw unto themselves the executive powers of Government I must observe to Your Lordships.

1stly That the Assembly refuse to admit of any amendment to any money bill, in any part of the Bill; so that the Bill must pass as it comes from the Assembly, or all the Supplies granted for the support of Government, & the most urgent services must be lost.

2ndly It appears that they take the Payment of the Forces, passing of Muster Rolls into their own hands by naming the Commissaries for those purposes in the Act.

3rdly They by granting the Saleries to the Officers personaly by name & not to the Officer for the time being, intimate that if any person be appointed to any Office his Salery must depend upon their approbation of the Appointment.

4thly They issue the greatest part of the Money granted to His Majesty without Warrant, though by His Majesty's Commission to me it is directed that all Monies raised by Act of Assembly, shall be issued from the Treasury by my Warrant & not otherwise.

5thly They have appointed an Agent for the Colony who is to take his Directions from a Committee of Assembly (exclusive of the Council & of the Governour) and to be paid by Warrant from the Speaker of the Assembly.

6thly In order to lay me under a necessity of passing the Bill for payment of the Officers Saleries & Services in the manner the Assembly had formed it, they tackt to it the payment of the Forces posted on the Frontier for the Defence thereof, so that I must either pass the Bill, or leave the Colony defenceless, & open to the Enemies incursions.

This last laid me under great difficulties, in refusing my Assent, & therefore I took the Advice of His Majesties Council for this Province, as to what may be proper for me to do on this occasion who advised me, from the present urgency of affairs, to give my assent to the Bill.

But as by the prospect of a General pacification I am in hopes to be freed from the difficulties the Assembly has from time to time (since the rupture with France) laid me under in their making Provision for the Defence of the Country: I must now referr it to Your Lordships consideration whether it be not high time to put a stop to these usurpations of the Assembly on His Majesty's Authority in this Province, and for that purpose may it not be proper that His Majesty signify his Disallowance of the Act at least for the payment of Saleries, though it have already in most parts taken its effect. There seems the more reason for this because the appointment of an Agent (exclusive of the Governour & Council) may be construed a perpetual clause, or at least may give ground for their insisting on the like clause in all future Acts of Assembly, & for their likewise insisting on the same Method of supporting the Government. And I must in General beg of Your Lordships to take under Your serious consideration what Instruction or other Method may be necessary to put a stop to these perpetually growing Incroachments of the Assemblies of this Province, on the executive Powers intrusted with me and his Majesty's other Officers. I am with the greatest regard,

My Lords,
Your Lordships most humble
and most obedient Servant

Fort George, at New York.   G. CLINTON.
20 October 1748.

To
   The Right Honorable The Lords Commissioners
   of Trade and Plantations.

29.—POLITICAL FRICTION:
SEABOARD VERSUS BACKCOUNTRY

Not all of Colonial America's political friction occurred between the colony and the mother country. Equally common were tensions between rival political factions within each colony or even between one colony and another. And often political tensions flared between the seaboard area— usually the more aristocratic and cosmopolitan section— and the backcountry. On the frontier a rougher breed of settler faced problems for which the more protected areas had little concern. Occasionally the backwoodsmen lost patience with government and took matters into their own hands—as in the incident described below by a Lutheran clergyman in Pennsylvania. The wrath of the frontiersmen,

*known as the "Paxton Boys," was in the end ameliorated
by Benjamin Franklin, who convinced them to present their
grievances to the Assembly.—From Theodore G. Tappert
and John W. Doberstein, eds.,* The Notebook of a Colonial
Clergyman *[Henry Melchior Muhlenberg] (Philadelphia,
1959), pp. 95-102.*

February 1 [1764]. This afternoon all citizens were summoned to
the state house by the governor and *counsel* through the *conestable.*
There the governor made a public proclamation:

(1) That it had been learned that a large mob of frontier settlers,
who had killed several Indians in Lancaster, were coming to Philadelphia to kill the Indian families who had been brought down from
Bethlehem and taken under the protection of the government.

(2) That since such procedure could be considered as being none
other than a breach of the peace, revolution, or rebellion against our
gracious king and the law of the land, the *Act of Riot* was invoked
and one hundred and some regular soldiers were set apart to guard
and protect the Bethlehem Indian families in the barracks.

(3) That the governor and *counsel* called upon citizens who were
willing to lend armed assistance and resist the rebellion to band
themselves together and hand in their names.

(4) That because there was a pouring rain at the time and the
Germans did not enlist and sign their names with the rest, the governor and others were much offended, conjecturing that perhaps the
Germans might be making common cause with the malcontents or so-
called rebels, etc.

As far as I can learn, the opinion and sentiment of various ones of
our German citizens is as follows:

(1) They were of the opinion that it could be proved that the
Indians who had lived among the so-called Moravian Brethren had
secretly killed several settlers.

(2) That the Quakers and Bethlehemites had only used some of
the aforesaid Indians as spies and that they had in view only their
own selfish interests, without considering at all that they had murdered their fellow Christians.

(3) Indeed, that they had loaded down the said Indians with
presents and taken them, their secret enemies, to their bosom only
for the sake of this selfish interest, which explained why the Quakers,
etc. in Philadelphia did not exhibit the least evidence of human
sympathy, etc. when Germans and other settlers on the frontiers were
massacred and destroyed in the most inhuman manner by the Indians.

On the contrary, these Bethlehem Indians, despite their congenital craftiness, etc., were brought to Philadelphia and maintained and supported at the expense of the inhabitants. Besides, the young male Indians had already escaped and were probably doing harm while the old men and women and children were living off the fat of the land at the expense of the province.

(4) And now because there was a rumor that the remote settlers, some of whom had lost their wives and others their children and relatives through these atrocious Indian massacres, were intending to come to Philadelphia in a corps and revenge themselves upon these Indians, and therefore our German citizens should enlist to fight, resist, or even kill their own flesh and blood, their fellow citizens and fellow Christians, and seek to protect the lives of the Bethlehem Indians! Why, they say, that would be quite contrary to nature and contrary to the law of Christ, for he did not say, "Thou shalt hate thy friend and love thine enemy." That is the general *tone* among some. They would unhesitatingly and gladly pour out their possessions and their blood for our most gracious king and his officers, but they would not wage war against their own suffering fellow citizens for the sake of the Quakers and Moravians and their creatures or instruments, the double-dealing Indians.

It is difficult in such a crisis to say anything or give any judgment in such a strange *republick* which has caught a fever, or, rather, is suffering from *colica pituitosa*.

February 5. Toward evening the rumor sprang up that a corps of backwoods settlers—Englishmen, Irishmen, and Germans—were on the march toward Philadelphia to kill the Bethlehem Indians at the barracks outside the city. Some reported that they numbered seven hundred, others said fifteen hundred, etc. The Friends, or so-called Quakers, and the Moravians ran furiously back and forth to the barracks, and there was a great to-do over constructing several small fortresses or ramparts near the barracks. Cannons were also set up. Some remarked concerning all this that it seemed strange that such preparations should be made against one's own fellow citizens and Christians, whereas no one ever took so much trouble to protect from the Indians His Majesty's subjects and citizens on the frontier.

• • •

After two o'clock at night the watchmen began to cry, "Fire!" I asked our watchman, who is a member of our congregation, where the fire was. He said there was no fire, but that the watchmen had orders to cry out, "Fire," because the above-mentioned backwoodsmen were approaching. Thereupon all the alarm bells began to ring at once and a drum was sounded to summon the inhabitants of the city to the town hall plaza. The ringing sounded dreadful in the night.

I asked a German neighbor to go to the town hall and bring me news of what was happening there. He reported that the market place was crowded with all sorts of people and that arms were being distributed to those who would take them. He had not, however, seen many Germans. The sounding of the tocsin continued on through the night until near dawn, and the inhabitants were ordered to place lights inside the doors and windows, which was done. Meanwhile, all sorts of rumors were flying in every direction: The rebels had divided into three groups and were going to attack the open city in three places simultaneously; then they were near; then they were still far away; now they were coming from the east, then from the west, and so on.

February 6. The alarm bells finally ceased at daylight. About nine o'clock Dr. Wrangel came and told us that he had been invited to attend upon the governor and *counseil* and that the *venerabile concilium* was annoyed because few or none of our German church people had reported on Saturday or last night to take up arms against the rebels, which might give rise to evil reflections, etc. Dr. Wrangel therefore felt himself compelled by motives of the common good, and especially the good of our German nation, to urge our Germans who had stood idly in the market place to take up arms. Because I was still weak from my illness and was unable to go out, Dr. Wrangel ordered Pastor Brycelius, who was still with me, to drive to Germantown with all haste and in our names (a) warn the elders of our congregation there not to join the approaching rebels, but rather to stand on the side of the government, and (b) since it had been bruited about that there were many Germans among the so-called rebels, Mr. Brycelius was to try and see whether he could not give them an earnest and kindly admonition, etc.

Dr. Wrangel left us and roused up a number of our Germans. Mr. Brycelius rode to Germantown because the word was going around that the mob was coming toward Germantown from Whitemarsh. Several hours later Mr. Metzger and other craftsmen gathered together, formed themselves into a small mounted company furnished with proper arms, sounded the trumpets, and made a several hours' tour in and around the city. They were almost shot by inadvertence, for cannons loaded with small balls had been placed here and there and the ignorant *constable* was just on the point of blazing away at them because he thought they were rebels. It seems almost inconceivable, but a number of older and younger Quakers also formed themselves into companies and took up arms, etc.

At any rate, it was a strange sight to the children on the streets. A whole *troup* of small boys followed a prominent Quaker down the street shouting in amazement, "Look, look! a Quaker carrying a musket on his shoulder!" Indeed, the older folks also looked upon it as a miraculous portent to see so many old and young Quakers arming themselves with flintlocks and daggers, or so-called murderous weapons! What heightened their amazement was this: that these pious sheep, who had had such a tender conscience during the long Spanish, French, and Indian War, and would rather have died than lift a hand for defense against the most dangerous enemies, were now all of a sudden willing to put on horns of iron like Zedekiah, the son of Chenaanah (I Kings 22), and shoot and smite a small group of their poor, oppressed, driven, and suffering fellow inhabitants and citizens from the frontier!

Pastor Brycelius returned from Germantown at evening and came to see me after having delivered his message to the governor. He reported what had happened, namely, that when he arrived in Germantown he had delivered the warning to the elders of our congregation, but they had not seen, nor did they know anything of, the so-called rebels. He therefore rode all the way through Germantown, over Chestnut Hill, and up to the point where the dwellings stop, and there he suddenly and unexpectedly ran into the vanguard of these people. He realized his mistake and was about to turn and flee, but he was stopped and ordered to remain with them.

• • •

. . . He innocently asked them what was the purpose of their coming. They replied that it was not their intention to do any injury to the least child of their fellow inhabitants nor to anyone else. It was rather their purpose:

(a) To demand the custody of the Bethlehem Indians, not to kill them, but only to conduct them out of the province; they were ready to put up a bond of ten thousand pounds that this was their intention.

(b) The people in and around Philadelphia lived a pleasant, protected life and had no feelings for the great need and tribulation which the poor settlers on the frontier had to endure. They lacked protection and even the barest necessities. So, since they had a number of weighty *gravamina* to present to the government, which must of necessity be redressed, they had set out on this journey to settle their grievance in Philadelphia.

Mr. Brycelius replied that it was his opinion that as far as their first point, regarding the Indians, was concerned, they would not achieve their purpose because of the following reasons:

(1) The government had taken these Indians under its protection, and after it had learned that a company was coming down with the intention of murdering them, just as they had murdered the Indians in Lancaster, it had on the past Saturday publicly proclaimed that this was a case of illegal assembly and forthwith the *Act of Riot* was read, declaring that if they did not desist they would be declared outlaws.

(2) Furthermore, the government had hired, from His Majesty's general, a large company of royal soldiers who were now under arms and guarding the remaining Indian families in the barracks. Yesterday (Sunday) the soldiers had completed a number of defenses and placed cannons in order to destroy any attack upon the barracks, etc. Besides these measures, as soon as word of their coming had arrived last night, the tocsin had been sounded and there had been a great mobilization of arms, etc. And now, since, by their own admission, they had already endured such great affliction and danger on the frontier, and their poor women and children who escaped the Indian massacres were still back at home, Mr. Brycelius said that he pitied their wretched and miserable condition from the bottom of his heart, but that he urgently begged them not to plunge further into utter destruction and not to take one step farther toward this *precipice*, but rather to commit their case into the hands of God and the government.

Regarding the second point, he said that he did not think it at all advisable that they should go to Philadelphia armed, inasmuch as this would cause a great and horrible blood-bath. They ought rather to send their most intelligent men into the city as unarmed deputies to the governor, and in this way, it was to be hoped,. their grievances would be remedied and under God's blessing peacefully settled.

All this appeared to give them pause and to make an *impression* on them. They replied that so far only two hundred and fifty of them had arrived and that they expected to have the rest of their comrades with them by twelve o'clock at night so that they would then number about fifteen hundred, although three thousand inhabitants had enlisted. At that time they would consider the matter further.

When Pastor Brycelius, with good intention, remarked to them, among other things, that even the Quakers had taken up arms, they laughed heartily and were amazed at such a *phenomenon*. Mr. Brycelius offered to give them something to drink for refreshment, but they refused absolutely to accept it, saying that they were used to nothing but the most extreme want. They had a rule among them that if anybody discharged a flintlock without a command, he was immediately to be shot by the person next to him. While Mr. Brycelius was there, a flintlock went off unexpectedly and the others immediately shouted, "Shoot him dead!" Several others, however, immediately objected that it had been done unintentionally. They were so trustful of Mr. Brycelius that they even gave him the password for the night. He therefore also asked them who their captain or leader was. But here they were shrewd and replied in the phraseology of the Indians that they were all brothers and that they also had among them some old persons whose advice they followed. After Mr. Brycelius had done what he could, besides the efforts made by two English preachers of the High Church and a Presbyterian professor from the Academy, who had likewise been requested by the governor to see what they could do among these people, he departed and returned to my house. He judged that there were very few Germans among them, that most of them were English and Scotch-Irish *dissenters*. For the rest, he said, they appeared to be resolute and soldier-like, but withal decent and substantial, most of them furnished with horses, muskets, a pair of pistols, and Indian hatchets.

Here in Philadelphia the militia drilled in the largest meeting house of the Quakers on the market place.

30.—THE ADMINISTRATION OF JUSTICE, AMERICAN-STYLE

There were few legal experts and many situations for which there was neither tested law nor clear precedent in British America. Not surprisingly then, English visitors often looked askance at colonial legal procedures—as reflected by this account of Boston's courts in 1740.—From Joseph Bennett, "History of New England," Proceedings of the Massachusetts Historical Society, 1 Ser. V (1860-62), 119-122.

As to the laws, if any one inquires after them, their lawyers say that the practice here is much the same as in England; but, upon attending their courts, they seem very different to what I have seen in England. Their trials by jury are all at bar: they have no such thing as *nisi prius**; nor do they make use of a book to swear either jury or witness on. Their manner of swearing their juries and witnesses is somewhat like our arraigning of prisoners. The officer that swears them first calls them by their names; and then, bidding them hold up their hands, he repeats the form of the oath to them (which differs also from ours): which being ended, the party lowers his hand to its proper place, and, without any other sign of assenting, is said to be sworn. Nor do the jury consider of their verdicts in every cause singly, as in England, but jumble six or seven of them together; and they will very frequently rise in the middle of a cause, if they are hungry at noon, or sleepy at night, and let the jury wander where they please, without taking the verdicts in those causes which they have gone through.

They have another method of practice that to me don't seem very agreeable: and that is, if any of their witnesses don't care for being present in court at the time of the trial of the cause, they take them before some justice of peace, where what they have to say is committed to writing, and sworn; and this is admitted as evidence, equal to the witnesses being present. This, in England, would be thought very strange practice, and big with great inconveniences, and more too, perhaps, than I am capable of apprehending; but, if such a custom was to prevail in England, there are some attorneys that would seldom want evidence sufficient to answer any end they had in view, if they could establish it with so much ease and privacy, without being examined or properly interrogated. But, if there was no other inconveniency than that of losing the benefit of cross-examination in court,—by which means not only the force of the evidence is much abated very often, but witnesses are more cautious of what they swear in the face of the country than when they do it in secret; nor would it be thought proper, in England, to acquaint a justice of peace with that which would be material evidence in a cause of any consequence, —these reasons already mentioned are therefore sufficient to show the danger and weakness of this sort of practice.

For the better security of their conveying their lands, mortgaging or otherwise alienating their several kinds of estates, there is an office kept in every county for the entering and enrolling the deeds, after

---

* In England, the central courts sat *en banc* only at Westminster, but individual judges periodically went on circuit to various counties to preside at the trial of causes where a jury was necessary. In Massachusetts, the Superior Court of Judicature sat *en banc* in each county in turn—ED.

the grantor has acknowledged them before some justice of peace; and this, they say, effectually prevents frauds in this respect. All kinds of their proceedings at law are, and ever were, in English, here; but, notwithstanding that, they make use of more technical words than the gentlemen in Westminster Hall. They litigate suits here very easy and cheap, compared with ours in England, for less than a tenth part of the cost at present; but how long it will remain so is something doubtful with me: of which, more anon.

• • •

The judges are not bound down by any strict rules of law, but are at liberty to make such equitable constructions as they think proper, in cases that require them so to do. They have a superior court; and also an inferior court, which is properly a court of common pleas; for, in this latter court, all suits in relation to right and property are commenced. But, from the judgment of this inferior court, they have a power of appealing to the court above; which originally was intended in extraordinary cases only, but now has become common: and from hence it is that I apprehend they may in time be led into great inconveniences and delays which will be prejudicial to them.

And, indeed, I think it's a great inconveniency to honest suitors already. For the inferior court, at this day, is little better than a stumbling-block in the road to justice; for, after a fruitless travelling through this court, which side soever the verdict goes against generally appeals to the court above, for the sake of delay, as writs of error are generally brought in England. But that which greatly contributes to delay here is, they have commonly a second hearing of the cause in the inferior court, before they remove it to the superior: and this second trial they call "reviewing of the cause;" but it is what is called, in England, "trying of the cause."

And when they come to the court above, after the cause has undergone a litigation there, then follows a second trial there also, which they also call "reviewing of the cause;" and thus three or four causes arise out of every one. By which means, it is commonly two years, and often longer, before any one can take the benefit of his suit, supposing death, nor any other accident, to befall the parties in the intervening space of time, which is possible there may; and, if it should so happen, the suitor is sure to be much longer delayed, if not totally deprived of his property in the end. There is another privilege they have, which, without doubt, was intended for their good, though commonly now made use of to oppress one another: I mean, that of appealing over to England to the King in Council, as it is called. I have heard many of them argued at the cockpit, when attending on my Lord Chief-Justice. This right of appealing does not extend to any thing in controversy that is under the value of four hundred pounds sterling; but they may, notwithstanding that, appeal over, by way of complaint, in lesser matters, where they suggest that justice has been denied them here. So that the above limitation is, in fact, no bar to any one appealing in the most trivial matters, if the expense is not too great; for it is easy to suggest the want of justice, when they know that will answer the end. This gives the rich, litigious man an opportunity to oppress his poor neighbor.

As to criminal matters, they are very tender in punishing of them; and very rarely put any to death, unless it be for murder. By their law, robbing on the highway, or burglary, for the first offence, branding on the forehead only; for the second offence, branding again and whipping; and, for the third offence, death. Blasphemy is punished with death. A child, for striking or cursing a parent, to be punished with death, if upwards of sixteen years of age. Cruel punishments or correction of either children, servants, or slaves, prohibited. Nor may any court of justice condemn any offender to receive more than forty stripes. No orphan may be disposed of by their guardian, without the consent of one of the courts. The minority of women, in respect of marriage, is determined to be under sixteen. They have many other laws relating to their religious and civil government; but I take those already mentioned to be the most material.

To the inferior court they have four judges, and to the superior court they have five judges. The reason they give me for their having five judges in the superior court is, that it prevents causes being hung up, by the judges being equally divided in their opinions in points of law; and they insist upon it, that we in England are defective in not having an odd one upon the bench, to prevent the like inconveniences. I do remember, indeed, that in our court of common pleas, in the reign of Edward III., the history of those times mentions nine justices to have been in that court at one time; in King John's time, six; and in Edward I.'s time, five. . . .

The judges here have no robes, nor other marks of distinction, to denote their dignity, nor officer of State of any kind whatsoever. Their judges' pay is exceedingly poor: it is no more than five hundred pounds per annum, of their currency; which is short of one hundred pounds sterling. There are no regular counsel at the bar; but the attorney, by the general appellation of "lawyer," conducts the cause from first to last. But, were you to hear them shriek and scream out their oratory before the court and jury, you would think they as well deserved to be compared with our solicitor-general, or some other of the first-rate gentlemen at the bar, as a common ballad-singer does with the celebrated Faranello.

They don't make up any record of the causes, as we do, at *nisi prius;* but the attorney reads the complaint contained in the declaration, and, at the same time, acquaints the court with the nature of the proof, and so proceed to give evidence. But notwithstanding they differ very much from what I have seen in the courts in England, yet I think the judges seem to aim at doing impartial justice between the contending parties, and hear both sides with all the temper and indulgence that possibly can be, so long as they have any thing to offer; and, if either the plaintiff or defendant think proper to say any thing in their own cause, the court never refuses to hear them, and all the judges sit in every cause.

VII

Arts
and Entertainment

In the seventeenth century Americans had little time for leisure.
The heavy demands of building homesteads, clearing land, planting fields, and warding off enemies kept artistic endeavor and or-
ganized entertainment to a minimum. But in the eighteenth century
Americans increasingly found opportunities for recreation and artistic
expression.

The pastimes of Colonial America were largely those that came
in the immigrants' cultural baggage. Games and sports that had been
enjoyed in the home countries remained the favorite forms of recrea-
tions in the New World. There were modifications, of course. Americans put greater emphasis on vigorous sports and on sports involving
weapons of war, and were also notoriously attached to games of
chance. The former were especially popular on the frontier, the latter
in the South. As a Bostonian visiting South Carolina observed,
somewhat uncharitably, "cards, dice, the bottle, and horses engross
prodigious portions of time and attention: the gentlemen (planters
and merchants) are mostly men of the turf and gamesters." But even
Boston had its share of gamblers and tipplers; cockfighting served
there as a partial substitute for horseracing. And throughout British
America, dancing, musical recitals, dress balls, and carriage rides
provided more polite forms of recreation.

On the other hand, the American colonies were largely bereft of
artistic culture in the half-century before the Revolutionary War.
There were only a handful of native architects, painters, and sculp-
tors. Among the painters only John Smibert, Robert Feke, and John
Singleton Copley still evoke admiration (Benjamin West, though

American, chose to live and paint in London) ; the work of Charles Willson Peale, John Trumbull, and Gilbert Stuart was yet to come. Peter Harrison and William Buckland had modest reputations as architects; the achievements of Charles Bulfinch, William Thornton, and Benjamin Latrobe were still a generation away. And it is perhaps symbolic that the only American sculptor of the Provincial period whose name is easily recognized is Shem Drowne, a designer of weathervanes. Rare, too, were writers of poetry and fictional prose. Mather Byles, Benjamin Church, and William Livingston enjoyed some recognition, but far more memorable are the writers of theology, history, and (increasingly in the 1760s and 1770s) of politics; and all of these considered themselves expostulators or recorders, not artists. There were almost no notable musicians, although an appreciation of music was becoming evident. Similarly, theatrical writers and actors were few, but here again appreciation was growing and some American productions had achieved a professional quality.

The one area in which Colonial America escapes charges of cultural deprivation is the practical crafts—pottery, metalwork (especially in silver and pewter), furniture design, and glassware. Few individual craftsmen are still well-known (silversmith Paul Revere's fame stems from other exploits), but the overall quality of their work is as widely recognized now as then. Unfortunately, there is little written description of American skill in handicrafts. Our knowledge of it rests on the few surviving items themselves.

If the arts and entertainment of pre-Revolutionary America were largely derivative, they were nonetheless a significant part of colonial society. In the half-century before the War for Independence Americans at last had opportunities for leisure and for cultural expression and appreciation. The forms they took and the advances made in them tell much about life in Colonial America.

31.—THE EMERGENCE
OF AN AMERICAN THEATER

From the time that the first American theater was erected in 1716 at Williamsburg, Virginia, the southern and middle colonies increasingly enjoyed theatrical performances. The one described below took place in the Philadelphia suburb

*of Southwark, where, judging from the reviewer's com-
ments, the audience was distinguished by its rudeness.—
From a copy at The New-York Historical Society.*

[From *The Pennsylvania Chronicle and Universal Advertiser,*
October 24-31, 1772]

On *Wednesday* last the THEATRE in *Southwark* was opened, by
the AMERICAN COMPANY, with *Kelly's Word to the Wise,* and
the *Padlock*; to a most crowded and brilliant Audience—The *Padlock*
we have, with Pleasure, seen many Repetitions of the last Season,
and Mr. *Hallam,* in *Mungo,* was, *then,* supposed excellent, but we,
now, upon the Judgment of Gentlemen of undoubted Knowledge and
Taste in Theatrical Performances, pronounce him to be the best
Mungo upon the *British* Stage; the other Characters, except *Leander,*
which we verily believe Mr. *Wall* does as well as he can, and therefore we must by no Means censure him, are well supported—The
Comedy we think is the best acting Sermon of Morality, we have
heard, and we sincerely congratulate the Friends of the Theatre,
upon the Chastity and Purity of our modern Comedies; where Vice,
if held up to public View at all, is shewn in so deformed, so ludicrous
a Light, that to see it, is sufficient to make us abhor and detest it;
and where Virtue appears dignified, by Sentiments that do Honour to
Humanity, and is beheld in every Light that can excite our Admiration—This we hope will entirely rescue the Theatre, "the noblest
Institution the Wit of Man ever designed," from the Contempt it has
been treated with, by many worthy, but mistaken, Persons, on Account of some Exuberances, which the present Taste of the Age has
"altogether reformed"—when the most virtuous can go to the Play-
House, without the least Apprehension of having "the Blush called
up into the Cheek of Modesty"—we flatter ourselves that the little
dirty commonplace Aspersions, with which the illiberal Hand of
Ignorance has so frequently larded it, will vanish; and we are bold
enough to say, that the Comedies of *Kelly, Cumberland, Colman,
Bickerstaff,* and many others, abound with Sentiments, Examples
and Characters, worthy our Adoption, Attention and Imitation.—
The Performers in the *Word to the Wise* are entitled to much Praise,
for being so correct, spirited, and characteristic—The Ladies, besides
their pleasing Figures, were genteel, elegant, and fashionable, in their
Deportment—Miss Hallam, in the sprightly Miss *Montagu,* was as
much a Woman of Fashion as we have seen on any Stage—But there

is one Grievance loudly to be complained of, and which *must* be remedied—Some Ruffians in the Gallery, who so frequently interrupted the Performance, and in the most interesting Scenes, deserve the severest Reprehension—they are too despicable to argue with, otherwise they might be told, that, because they pay Three Shillings for their Admittance into a public Assembly, they are not, therefore, warranted to commit repeated Outrages, upon that Part of the Audience who go there really to see the Play, and be instructed and entertained; or to interrupt the Actors who are doing their best to please them—They might be informed, that, tho' they have an undoubted Right to every Species of Entertainment, promised them in the Bills, they have not the smallest Title to any Thing else, and that if they call for a Song, or a Prologue, of which no Notice is given in the Bills, the Actors have an equal Demand upon them for an extraordinary Price for a Compliance with their Request—which of those vociferous Gentlemen, if a Carpenter, Mason, or Taylor, will do more Work than he bargains for without an adequate Compensation?—Are not the Players in the same Predicament.—But to dismiss the Subject, the Directors of the Theatre are thus publicly desired to engage a Number of Constables, and dispose them in different Parts of the Gallery, who upon the smallest Disturbance, for the Future, may be authorized, by any Magistrate, and there are always enough in the House, to apprehend, and carry to the Work-house, such Rioters, by which Means, Peace will be restored, and a few Examples deter others from the like Outrages.

I am, Sir, your humble Servant,

Oct. 30, 1772.   PHILO-THEATRICUS.

32.— CULTURE AND DIVERSION IN THE CITIES

The following accounts reflect the cultural interests and leisure pastimes of two Colonial American cities. The first was written in 1773 by Josiah Quincy, Jr., of Massachusetts during a visit to Charleston, South Carolina. The second dates from 1740 when an Englishman, Joseph Bennett, recorded his impressions of Boston.—From Mark A.

D. Howe, ed., "Journal of Josiah Quincy, Junior, 1773,"
Proceedings of the Massachusetts Historical Society, XLIX
(1915-16), 441-446, 448, 451; and from Joseph Bennett,
"History of New England," Proceedings of the Massachusetts Historical Society, 1 Ser. V (1860-62), 124-126.

[Quincy]

March 2. This day I was waited upon by several gentleman to
whom yesterday I had delivered letters. Those who came in my absence left cards with their names. Received a ticket from David Deis,
Esquire, for the St. Cecilia Concert, and now quit my journal to go.

March 3. The Concert-house is a large inelegant building situated down a yard at the entrance of which I was met by *a Constable with his staff.* I offered him my ticket, which was *subscribed
by the name of the person giving it,* and directing admission of me
by name, the officer told me to proceed. I did and was next met by
a white waiter, who directs me to a third to whom I delivered my
ticket and was conducted in. The Hall is preposterously and out of
all proportion large, no orchestra for the performers, though a kind
of loft for fiddlers at the Assembly. The performers were all at one
end of the hall and the company in front and on each side. The musick was good. The two bass-viols and French horns were grand.
One Abbercrombie, a Frenchman just arrived, played a first fiddle
and solo incomparably, better than any I ever had heard: I have
several times heard John Turner and Morgan play a solo. Abbercrombie can't speak a word of English and has a salary of 500
guineas a year from the St. Cecilia Society. Hartley was here, and
played as I thought badly on the harpsischord. The capital defect
of this concert was want of an organ.

• • •

In loftiness of head-dress these ladies stoop to the daughters of the
North: in richness of dress surpass them: in health and floridity of
countenance veil to them: in taciturnity during the performances
greatly before our ladies: in noise and flirtations after the music is
over pretty much on a par. If our Women have any advantage it
is in white and red, vivacity and fire.

The gentlemen many of them dressed with richness and elegance
uncommon with us—many with swords on. We had two Macaronis
present—just arrived from London. This character I found real, and

not fictitious. "See the Macaroni," was common phrase in the hall.
One may well be stiled the Bag—and the other the Cue-Macaroni.

*   *   *

March 3. Spent in viewing horses, riding over the town and
into the vicinity, and receiving formal complements.

March 4, Thursday. Dined with four other Gentlemen with David
Deis, Esq. Table decent and not inelegant: provisions indifferent,
but well dressed: no apology: good wines and festivity. Salt fish
brought in small bits in a dish made a corner. The first toast, the
king: the second, a lady: the third, our friends at Boston and your
(meaning my) fire-side. The master of the feast then called to the
gentleman on his right hand *for a lady:* this was done to every one,
except to the ladies at table (Mr. D's daughters about sixteen and
eighteen) who were called upon for a *gentleman* and gave one with
ease. The ladies withdrew after the first round—the father seemed
displeased at it. Glasses were changed every time different wine was
filled. A sentiment was given by each gentleman and then we were
called to coffee and tea. No compulsion in drinking, except that a
bumper was called for at the third toast. Politicks an uninteresting
topick.

March 5, Friday. Dined at a very elegantly disposed and plentiful table at the house of John Matthews Esqr (son in law of Col.
Scott) in company with the Chief Justice of St. Augustine, and several other gentlemen. Puddings and pies brought in hot after meats
taken away. The flour of the place in general is indifferent. First
toast, The King and his friends. The master of the feast calls upon
his lady for a *gentleman* as a second toast—given with ease. Ladies
go round as toasts. The females withdraw, and sentiments succeed.
No compulsion in drinking: no interesting conversation. Good wines.

March 6. This day was to have been spent with Thomas Lough-
ton Smith Esqr. at his country seat. Bad weather prevents, and I
take what is called a family dinner with him. A prodigious fine
pudding made of what they call rice flour. Nicknacks brought on
table after removal of meats. Ladies ask the gentlemen to drink a
glass of wine with them: Upon a gentleman's asking a lady to do
the like, she replies "G— bless you, I thought you never would ask.
I have been waiting for you this half hour."

First toast, Our Boston friend and your good health. Sir: the
unmarried lady (of nineteen) at my right, "your good health and
best affections Sir!" Miss —— your toast, madam. "Love and friendship and they who feel them!" Toasts called for from the guests, etc.,
till coffee, etc. Mr. Smith's house furniture, pictures, plate etc. very

elegant—wines very fine. Mrs. Smith shewed me a most beautiful white satin and very richly embroidered lady's work-bag, designed as a present for a lady in London. Miss Catherine Ingliss, her sister, a still more finely embroidered festoon (as they called it) of flowers. Both their own work; and far surpassing anything of the kind I ever saw.

Before dinner a short account of the late disputes with the Governor Lord Charles G. Montague, and the state of matters at present. No politicks after dinner.

• • •

March 7. Dined with considerable company at Miles Brewton, Esqr's, a gentleman of very large fortune: a most superb house said to have cost him 8000£ sterling. The grandest hall I ever beheld, azure blue satin window curtains, rich blue paper with gilt, mashee borders, most elegant pictures, excessive grand and costly looking glasses etc. . . .

• • •

A most elegant table, three courses, nick-nacks, jellies, preserves, sweetmeats, etc.

After dinner, two sorts of nuts, almonds, raisins, three sorts of olives, apples, oranges, etc.

By odds the richest wine I ever tasted: Exceeds Mr. Hancock's, Vassall's, Phillips's and others much in flavour, softness, and strength.

I toast all your friends, Sir. Each gentleman gave his toast round in succession.

• • •

At Mr. Brewton's side board was very magnificent plate: a very large exquisitely wrought Goblet, most excellent workmanship and singularly beautiful.

A very fine bird kept familiarly playing over the room, under our chairs and the table, picking up the crumbs, etc., and perching on the window, side board and chairs: vastly pretty!

• • •

March 9. Dined with Mr. Thomas Smith; several gentlemen and ladies: decent and plenteous table of meats: the upper cloth removed, a compleat table of puddings, pies, tarts, custards, sweetmeats, oranges, macarones, etc., etc.—profuse. Excellent wines—no politicks.

March 10. Evening. Spent the evening at the Assembly. Bad musick, good dancing, elegantly disposed supper, bad provisions, worse dressed.

March 11. Dined with Mr. Roger Smith, son to Mr. Thomas Smith: good deal of company, elegant table, and the best provisions

I have seen in this town. One cloth removed, a handsome desert of most kinds of nicknacks. Good wines and much festivity. Two ladies being called on for toasts, the one gave, "Delicate pleasures to susceptable minds." The other, "When passions rise may reason be the guide."

• • •

March 15. Spent the evening with Monday-night Club; introduced to Mr. Brewton. Cards, feasting, and indifferent wines.

N.B. This was at a tavern, and was the first time of my meeting with ordinary wines since my being at Charlestown.

March 16. Spent this morning ever since five o'clock in perusing Public Records of the Province which I was favored with by the worthy Mr. Bee: have marked many to be copied for me. Am now going to the famous Races.

The races were well performed, but Flimnap beat Little David (who had won the sixteen last races) out and out. The last heat the former distanced the latter. The first four miles heat was performed in eight minutes and seventeen seconds, being four miles. 2000£ sterling was won and lost at the Race, and Flimnap sold at Public Vendue the same day for £300 Sterling. . . .

At the races I saw a prodigious fine collection of excellent, though very high-priced horses—and was let a little into the singular art of the Turf.

March 17. Spent all the morning in copying Mr. Rutledge's Reports. Feasted with the Sons of St. Patrick. While at dinner six violins, two hautboys and bassoon, with a hand-taber beat excellently well. After dinner six French horns in concert—most surpassing musick! Two solos on the French horn by one who is said to blow the finest horn in the world: he has fifty guineas for the season from the St. Cecilia Society.

∾

[Bennett]

Of their Cattle for the Coach,
Saddle, and Ordinary Draught;
with their Manner of Travelling,
Diversions, and Amusements.

There are several families in Boston that keep a coach, and pair of horses, and some few drive with four horses; but for chaises and saddle-horses, considering the bulk of the place, they outdo London. They have some nimble, lively horses for the coach, but not any of that beautiful large black breed so common in London. Their saddle-horses all pace naturally, and are generally counted sure-footed; but they are not kept in that fine order as in England. The common draught-horses used in carts about the town are very small and poor, and seldom have their fill of any thing but labor. The country carts and wagons are generally drawn by oxen, from two to six, according to the distance of place, or burden they are laden with. When the ladies ride out to take the air, it is generally in a chaise or chair, and then but a single horse; and they have a negro servant to drive them. The gentlemen ride out here as in England, some in chairs, and others on horseback, with their negroes to attend them. They travel in much the same manner on business as for pleasure, and are attended in both by their black equipages. Their roads, though they have no turnpikes, are exceeding good in summer; and it is safe travelling night or day, for they have no highway robbers to interrupt them. It is pleasant riding through the woods; and the country is pleasantly interspersed with farm-houses, cottages, and some few gentlemen's seats, between the towns. But the best of their inns, and houses of entertainment, are very short of the beauty and conveniences of ours in England. They have generally a little rum to drink, and some of them have a sorry sort of Madeira wine. And to eat they have Indian corn roasted, and bread made of Indian meal, and sometimes a fowl or fish dressed after a fashion, but pretty good butter, and very sad sort of cheese; but those that are used to those things think them tolerable.

For their domestic amusements, every afternoon, after drinking tea, the gentlemen and ladies walk the Mall, and from thence adjourn to one another's houses to spend the evening,—those that are not disposed to attend the evening lecture; which they may do, if they please, six nights in seven, the year round.

What they call the Mall is a walk on a fine green Common adjoining to the south-west side of the town. It is near half a mile over, with two rows of young trees planted opposite to each other, with a fine footway between, in imitation of St. James's Park; and part of the bay of the sea which encircles the town, taking its course along the north-west side of the Common,—by which it is bounded on the one side, and by the country on the other,—forms a beautiful canal, in view of the walk.

Their rural diversions are chiefly shooting and fishing. For the former, the woods afford them plenty of game; and the rivers and ponds with which this country abounds yield them great plenty, as well as variety, of fine fish.

The government being in the hands of dissenters, they don't admit of plays or music-houses; but, of late, they have set up an assembly, to which some of the ladies resort. But they are looked upon to be none of the nicest in regard to their reputation; and it is thought it will soon be suppressed, for it is much taken notice of and exploded by the religious and sober part of the people. But, notwithstanding plays and such like diversions do not obtain here, they don't seem to be dispirited nor moped for want of them; for both the ladies and gentlemen dress and appear as gay, in common, as courtiers in England on a coronation or birthday. And the ladies here visit, drink tea, and indulge every little piece of gentility, to the height of the mode; and neglect the affairs of their families with as good a grace as the finest ladies in London.

33.—SOCIAL LIFE
ON A VIRGINIA PLANTATION

The journal of Philip Fithian is replete with information about plantation life in the 1770s. In the selection below the young tutor describes one of the private balls frequently held by Virginia aristocrats—in this case by Richard Lee. —From John Rogers Williams, ed., Philip Vickers Fithian: Journal and Letters, 1767-1774 *(Princeton, 1900), pp. 94-98.*

Monday 17. At Breakfast the Colonel gave orders to the Boys concerning their conduct this Day, & through the course of the Ball —He allows them to go; to stay all this Night; to bring him an Account of all the Company at the Ball; & to return to-morrow Evening—All the morning is spent in Dressing.—Mr. Carter & Mrs. Carter pressed me to go; But, mindful of my Promise when I left Home, I stay and enjoy myself in quiet.—I give the Children a Holiday to Day—I gave Dennis the Waiter half a Bit a Present— Mrs. *Carter,* Miss *Prissy* & *Nancy* dressed splendidly set away from Home at two.

Teusday 18. Mrs. *Carter,* & the young Ladies came Home last

Night from the Ball, & brought with them Mrs. *Lane,* they tell us
there were upwards of Seventy at the Ball; forty-one Ladies; that
the company was genteel; & that Colonel *Harry Lee,* from *Dumfries,*
& his Son *Harry* who was with me at College, were also there; Mrs.
Carter made this an argument, and it was a strong one indeed, that
to-day I must dress & go with her to the Ball—She added also that
She desired my Company in the Evening when she should come
Home as it would be late—After considering a while I consented to
go, & was dressed—we set away from Mr. Carters at two; Mrs.
Carter & the young Ladies in the Chariot, Mrs. Lane in a Chair, &
myself on Horseback—As soon as I had handed the Ladies out, I
was saluted by Parson *Smith;* I was introduced into a small Room
where a number of Gentlemen were playing Cards (the first game
I have seen since I left Home) to lay off my Boots Riding-Coat &c.
—Next I was directed into the Dining-Room to see young Mr. *Lee;*
He introduced me to his Father—With them I conversed til Dinner,
which came in at half after four. The Ladies dined first, when some
Good Order was preserved; when they rose, each nimblest Fellow
dined first—The Dinner was as elegant as could be well expected
when so great an Assembly were to be kept for so long a time.—For
Drink, there was several sorts of Wine, good Lemon Punch, Toddy,
Cyder, Porter &c.—About Seven the Ladies & Gentlemen begun to
dance in the Ball-Room—first Minuets one Round; Second Giggs;
third Reels; And last of All Country-Dances; tho' they struck several
Marches occasionally—The Music was a French-Horn and two Violins—The Ladies were Dressed Gay, and splendid, & when dancing,
their Skirts & Brocades rustled and trailed behind them!—But all
did not join in the Dance for there were parties in Rooms made up,
some at Cards; some drinking for Pleasure; some toasting the Sons
of america; some singing "Liberty Songs" as they call'd them, in
which six, eight, ten or more would put their Heads near together
and roar, & for the most part as unharmonious as an affronted—
Among the first of the Vociferators was a young Scotch-Man, Mr.
Jack Cunningham; he was nimis bibendo appotus; noisy, droll, wag-
gish, yet civil in his way & wholly inoffensive—I was solicited to
dance by several, Captain Chelton, Colonel Lee, Harry Lee, and
others; But George Lee with great Rudeness as tho' half drunk,
asked me why I would come to the Ball & neither dance nor play
Cards? I answered him shortly, (for his Impudence moved my re-
sentment) that my Invitation to the Ball would Justify my Presence;
& that he was ill qualified to direct my Behaviour who made so indifferent a Figure himself—Parson Smiths, & Parson Gibberns Wives

danced, but I saw neither of the Clergymen dance or game—At Eleven Mrs. Carter call'd upon me to go, I listened with gladness to the summons & with Mrs. Lane in the Chariot we rode Home, the Evening sharp and cold!—I handed the Ladies out, waited on them to a warm Fire, then ran over to my own Room, which was warm and had a good Fire; oh how welcome! Better this than to be at the Ball in some corner nodding, and awaked now & then with a midnight Yell!—In my Room by half after twelve; & exceeding happy that I could break away with Reputation.

Wednesday 19. Rose at Nine while the Bell was ringing—Breakfasted at ten, Mrs. *Carter* and I alone, the Ladies yet in Bed—I gave the Children the third Holiday; *Bob Ben & Harry* are yet at the Dance—Mrs. Carter declines going to Day. . . . *Bob* came Home about six, but so sleepy that he is actually stupified!

Thursday 20. Ben came Home late in the Night—This morning he looks fatigued out. We began to study to Day but all seem sleepy and dull. . . .

Fryday 21. All seem tolerably recruited this morning; we hear, the company left the Ball last Evening quite wearied out; tho' the Colonel intreated them to stay the proposed Time.

34.—FRONTIER PASTIMES

There were no opportunities for carriage rides or concerts or dress balls on the frontier. Yet those who lived on the western edge of civilization knew how to turn common events into festivals and necessary activities into sports. The following recollections of back-country recreation are from the memoirs of a man who spent his boyhood on the Pennsylvania frontier.—From Joseph Doddridge, Notes on the Settlement and Indian Wars . . . *(Pittsburgh, 1912), pp. 102-106, 122-125.*

In the first years of the settlement of this country [the Virginia-Pennsylvania frontier] a wedding engaged the attention of a whole neighborhood; and the frolic was anticipated by old and young with eager expectation. This is not to be wondered at, when it is told that a wedding was almost the only gathering which was not accompanied with the labor of reaping, log rolling, building a cabin, or planning some scout or campaign.

In the morning of the wedding day the groom and his attendants assembled at the house of his father for the purpose of reaching the mansion of his bride by noon, which was the usual time for celebrating the nuptials, which for certain must take place before dinner.

Let the reader imagine an assemblage of people without a store, tailor or mantuamaker [dressmaker] within a hundred miles; and an assemblage of horses without a blacksmith or saddler within an equal distance. The gentlemen dressed in shoepacks [leather shoes similar to moccasins], moccasins, leather breeches, leggins, linsey [coarse linen] hunting shirts, and all home made. The ladies dressed in linsey petticoats and linsey or linen bed gowns, coarse shoes, stockings, handkerchiefs and buckskin gloves, if any. If there were any buckles, rings, buttons, or ruffles, they were the relics of old times; family pieces from parents or grand parents. The horses were caparisoned with old saddles, old bridles or halters, and packsaddles, with a bag or blanket thrown over them: a rope or string as often constituted the girth as a piece of leather.

The march, in double file, was often interrupted by the narrowness and obstructions of our horse paths, as they were called, for we had no roads; and these difficulties were often increased, sometimes by the good, and sometimes by the ill will of neighbors, by felling trees and tying grape vines across the way. Sometimes an ambuscade was formed by the way side, and an unexpected discharge of several guns took place, so as to cover the wedding company with smoke. Let the reader imagine the scene which followed this discharge; the sudden spring of the horses, the shrieks of the girls, and the chivalric bustle of their partners to save them from falling. Sometimes, in spite of all that could be done to prevent it, some were thrown to the ground. If a wrist, elbow, or ankle happened to be sprained it was tied with a handkerchief, and little more was thought or said about it.

Another ceremony commonly took place before the party reached the house of the bride, after the practice of making whiskey began, which was at an early period. When the party were about a mile from the place of their destination, two young men would single out to run for the bottle; the worse the path, the more logs, brush and deep hollows the better, as these obstacles afforded an opportunity for the greater display of intrepidity and horsemanship. The English fox chase, in point of danger to the riders and their horses, is nothing to this race for the bottle. The start was announced by an Indian yell; logs, brush, muddy hollows, hill and glen, were speedily passed by the rival ponies. The bottle was always filled for the occasion, so that there was no use for judges; for the first who reached the door was presented with the prize, with which he returned in triumph to the company. On approaching them he announced his victory over his rival by a shrill whoop. At the head of the troop, he gave the bottle first to the groom and his attendants, and then to each pair in succession to the rear of the line, giving each a dram; and then, putting the bottle in the bosom of his hunting shirt, took his station in the company.

The ceremony of the marriage preceded the dinner, which was a substantial backwoods feast of beef, pork, fowls, and sometimes venison and bear meat roasted and boiled, with plenty of potatoes, cabbage, and other vegetables. During the dinner the greatest hilarity always prevailed; although the table might be a large slab of timber, hewed out with a broad axe, supported by four sticks set in auger holes; and the furniture, some old pewter dishes and plates; the rest, wooden bowls and trenchers; a few pewter spoons, much battered about the edges, were to be seen at some tables. The rest were made of horns. If knives were scarce, the deficiency was made up by the scalping knives which were carried in sheaths suspended to the belt of the hunting shirt.

After dinner the dancing commenced, and generally lasted till the next morning. The figures of the dances were three and four handed reels, or square sets and jigs. The commencement was always a square four, which was followed by what was called jigging it off; that is, two of the four would single out for a jig, and were followed by the remaining couple. The jigs were often accompanied with what was called cutting out; that is, when either of the parties became tired of the dance, on intimation, the place was supplied by some one of the company without any interruption of the dance. In this way a dance was often continued till the musician was heartily tired of his situation. Toward the latter part of the night, if any of the company, through weariness, attempted to conceal themselves for the purpose of sleeping, they were hunted up, paraded on the floor, and the fiddler ordered to play "Hang on till to-morrow morning."

About nine or ten o'clock a deputation of the young ladies stole off the bride and put her to bed. In doing this it frequently happened that they had to ascend a ladder instead of a pair of stairs, leading from the dining and ball room to the loft, the floor of which was made of clapboards lying loose and without nails. This ascent, one might think, would put the bride and her attendants to the blush; but as the foot of the ladder was commonly behind the door, which was purposely opened for the occasion, and its rounds at the inner end were well hung with hunting shirts, petticoats, and other articles of clothing, the candles being on the opposite side of the house, the exit of the bride was noticed but by few. This done, a deputation of young men in like manner stole off the groom, and placed him snugly by the side of his bride. The dance still continued; and if seats happened to be scarce, which was often the case, every young man, when not engaged in the dance, was obliged to offer his lap as a seat for one of the girls; and the offer was sure to be accepted. In the midst of this hilarity the bride and groom were not forgotten. Pretty late in the night some one would remind the company that the new couple must stand in need of some refreshment; black Betty, which was the name of the bottle, was called for and sent up the ladder, but sometimes black Betty did not go alone; I have many times seen as much bread, beef, pork and cabbage sent along with her as would afford a good meal for a half dozen hungry men. The young couple were compelled to eat and drink, more or less, of whatever was offered them.

In the course of the festivity if any wanted to help himself to a dram, and the young couple to a toast, he would call out:

"Where is black Betty? I want to kiss her sweet lips." Black Betty was soon handed to him. Then holding her up in his right hand he would say:

"Health to the groom, not forgetting myself; and here's to the bride, thumping luck and big children."

This, so far from being taken amiss, was considered as an expression of a very proper and friendly wish, for big children, especially sons, were of great importance; as we were few in number, and engaged in perpetual hostility with the Indians, the end of which no one could foresee. Indeed many of them seemed to suppose that war was the natural state of man, and therefore did not anticipate any conclusion of it; every big son was therefore considered as a young soldier.

But to return. It often happened that some neighbors or relations, not being asked to the wedding, took offense; and the mode of revenge adopted by them on such occasions was that of cutting off the manes, foretops and tails of the horses of the wedding company. Another method of revenge which was adopted when the chastity of the bride was a little suspected was that of setting up a pair of horns on poles, or trees, on the route of the wedding company. This was a hint to the groom that he might expect to be complimented with a pair of horns himself.

On returning to the infare, the order of procession and the race for black Betty was the same as before. The feasting and dancing often lasted for several days, at the end of which the whole company were so exhausted with loss of sleep that several days' rest were requisite to fit them to return to their ordinary labors.

• • •

Many of the sports of the early settlers of this country were imitative of the exercises and stratagems of hunting and war. Boys were taught the use of the bow and arrow at an early age. . . .

• • •

[Another] important pastime of our boys was that of imitating the noise of every bird and beast in the woods. This faculty was not merely a pastime, but a very necessary part of education, on account of its utility in certain circumstances. The imitations of the gobbling and other sounds of wild turkeys often brought those keen eyed and ever watchful tenants of the forest within the reach of the rifle. The bleating of the fawn brought her dam to her death in the same way. The hunter often collected a company of mopish owls to the trees about his camp, and amused himself with their hoarse screaming; his howl would raise and obtain responses from a pack of wolves, so as to inform him of their neighborhood, as well as guard him against their depredations.

• • •

Throwing the tomahawk was another boyish sport, in which many acquired considerable skill. The tomahawk with its handle of a certain length will make a given number of turns in a given distance. Say in five steps it will strike with the edge, the handle downwards; at the distance of seven and a half, it will strike with the edge, the handle upwards, and so on. A little experience enabled the boy to measure the distance with his eye, when walking through the woods, and strike a tree with his tomahawk in any way he chose.

The athletic sports of running, jumping and wrestling, were the pastimes of boys, in common with the men. A well grown boy, at the age of twelve or thirteen years, was furnished with a small rifle and shot pouch. He then became a fort soldier, and had his port hole assigned him. Hunting squirrels, turkeys and raccoons soon made him expert in the use of his gun.

Dancing was the principal amusement of our young people of both sexes. Their dances, to be sure, were of the simplest forms. Three and four handed reels and jigs. Contra dances, cotillions and minuets, were unknown. I remember to have seen, once or twice, a dance which was called the Irish trot, but I have long since forgotten its figure.

Shooting at marks was a common diversion among the men, when their stock of ammunition would allow it; this, however, was far from being always the case. . . . Their shooting was from a rest, and at as great distance as the length and weight of the barrel of the gun would throw a ball on a horizontal level. Such was their regard to accuracy, in these sportive trials of their rifles, and of their own skill in the use of them, that they often put moss, or some other soft substance, on the log or stump from which they shot, for fear of having the bullet thrown from the mark, by the spring of the barrel. When the rifle was held to the side of a tree for a rest, it was pressed against it as lightly as possible, for the same reason.

• • •

Dramatic narrations, chiefly concerning Jack and the giant, furnished our young people with another source of amusement during their leisure hours. Many of these tales were lengthy, and embraced a considerable range of incident. Jack, always the hero of the story, after encountering many difficulties, and performing many great achievements, came off conqueror of the giant. Many of these stories were tales of knight errantry, in which some captive virgin was released from captivity and restored to her lover. These dramatic narrations concerning Jack and the giant bore a strong resemblance to the poems of Ossian, the story of the Cyclops and Ulysses, in the Odyssey of Homer, and the tale of the giant and Great-heart, in the *Pilgrim's Progress*. They were so arranged, as to the different incidents of the narration, that they were easily committed to memory. . . .

• • •

Singing was another, but no very common, amusement among our first settlers. Their tunes were rude enough, to be sure. Robin Hood furnished a number of our songs, the balance were mostly tragical. These last were denominated "love songs about murder;" as to cards, dice, back-gammon and other games of chance, we knew nothing about them. These are amongst the blessed gifts of civilization.

35.—THE KING OF SPORTS

Horse racing was the favorite sport throughout the southern colonies; travelers reported it to be almost a mania in

Virginia. In 1772 Englishman J. F. D. Smyth visited the colonies and later published his impressions of the most popular American pastime.—From J. F. D. Smyth, A Tour in the United States of America *... (London, 1784), I, pp. 20-23.*

There are races at Williamsburg twice a year; that is, every spring and fall, or autumn. Adjoining to the town is a very excellent course, for either two, three or four mile heats. Their purses are generally raised by subscription, and are gained by the horse that wins two four-mile heats out of three; they amount to an hundred pounds each for the first day's running, and fifty pounds each every day after; the races commonly continuing for a week. There are also matches and sweepstakes very often, for considerable sums. Besides these at Williamsburg, there are races established annually, almost at every town and considerable place in Virginia; and frequent matches, on which large sums of money depend; the inhabitants, almost to a man, being quite devoted to the diversion of horse-racing.

Very capital horses are started here, such as would make no despicable figure at Newmarket; nor is their speed, bottom, or blood inferior to their appearance; the gentlemen of Virginia sparing no pains, trouble or expence in importing the best stock, and improving the excellence of the breed by proper and judicious crossing.

Indeed nothing can be more elegant and beautiful than the horses bred here, either for the turf, the field, the road, or the coach; and they have always fine, long, full, flowing tails; but their carriage horses seldom are possessed of that weight and power, which distinguish those of the same kind in England.

Their stock is from old Cade, old Crab, old Partner, Regulus, Babraham, Bosphorus, Devonshire Childers, the Cullen Arabian, the Cumberland Arabian, &c. in England; and a horse from Arabia, named the Bellsize, which was imported into America, and is now in existence.

In the southern part of the colony, and in North Carolina, they are much attached to *quarter-racing,* which is always a match between two horses, to run one quarter of a mile streight out, being merely an excursion of speed; and they have a breed that perform it with astonishing velocity, beating every other, for that distance, with great ease; but they have no bottom. However, I am confident that there is not a horse in England, nor perhaps the whole world, that can excel them in rapid speed; and these likewise make excellent saddle horses for the road.

The Virginians, of all ranks and denominations, are excessively fond of horses, and especially those of the race breed. The gentlemen of fortune expend great sums on their studs, generally keeping handsome carriages, and several elegant sets of horses, as well as others for the race and road: even the most indigent person has his saddlehorse, which he rides to every place, and on every occasion; for in this country nobody walks on foot the smallest distance, except when hunting: indeed a man will frequently go five miles to catch a horse, to ride only one mile upon afterwards. In short, their horses are their pleasure, and their pride.

36.—A GROWING APPRECIATION
OF LITERATURE AND ART

Although the books produced in Colonial America were predominantly didactic, some native literature and much of the imported literature served more casual purposes. At the same time, Americans were beginning to patronize craftsmen who combined aesthetic merit with practicality. The following newspaper advertisements reveal the eighteenth century American's taste in a variety of cultural forms.— From originals and photocopies at The New-York Historical Society.

[From *The Maryland Gazette*, February 10, 1757]

The following BOOKS being Lent to my *Friends*, some a longer and some a shorter Time, those who *think it Time* are requested to return them, the Proprietor being deprived of the Satisfaction of looking into them on Occasion, as well as of the Pleasure of *obliging Others* with their Perusal. Also he will be obliged to any Persons, who, finding any Book in their Possession, not here listed, with his Name prefix'd, shall send it home, and he will not murmur at the Expence of this Advertisement: Even though any of them should be much abused, according to Custom, they will yet be acceptable. To shew the Reasonableness of this Remark; I had not long ago return'd the ART OF COOKERY, in such a *Pickle* that one would

imagine it had been several Times in the *Pot* to make *Soups,* as they
use the Gusting-Bone in *Gallway.*

H. CALLISTER.

Swift's Works,	12 *mo.*	Vols.	7. 8. 9.
Clarissa,	12 *mo.*		1. 2. 3.
Independent Whig,	8 *vo.*		1. 2.
Bolingbroke,	4 *to.*		2. 3.
Louis de Bourbon, French,	12 *mo.*		2. or 3.
Cadwallader Colden's 5 Nations,	8 *vo.*		1.

[From *The Boston Evening Post,* April 3, 1738]

Thursday next, the 30th Instant,

Will be sold by publick Vendue at the Heart and
Crown *in* Cornhill, *a very neat Collection of*
BOOKS, being the Library of John Eastwicke,
Esq; late of Boston, *deceased, all in* English,
generally well bound, and many of them new;
among which are these following, viz.

Pool's Annotations, latest Edit.
Collier's Dictionary
Harris's Voyages
Homer's Iliads
Tillotson's Works, 3 Vols.
Camden's Britannia, 2 Vols.
Mather's Magnalia Christi Americ.
Rapin's Hist. of *England,* 7 Vols.
Clarendon's Hist. Rebellion, 6 Vols.
Plutarch's Lives, 8 Vols.
Echard's Roman History, 5 Vols.

Seneca's Morals
Athenian Oracle, 3 Vols.
Life of Q. *Anne,* 2 Vols.
Gentleman instructed
Bond's Justice
Spectators, 8 Vols.
Ray's Travels and Voyages.
Miscellanea Curiosa, 3 Vols.
Montaigne's Essays
Ductor Historicus, 2 Vols.

[From the *Pennsylvania Gazette,* March 15, 1759]

Lately imported from London, and to be sold by
DAVID HALL,

At the New-Printing-Office, in Market-street, a valuable
Collection of Books, amongst which are the following.

FOLIO'S.

BASKETS Bibles; large and small; Wood's Institutes, Modern Builder's Assistant; Burkitt on the New-Testament; Drummond's Travels; Gibb's Rules of Drawing; Streights and Mediterranean Pilot; West-India Ditto, and Supplement to Chamber's Dictionary.

QUARTO'S.

Bibles; Shaw's Boerhaave's Chymistry; Milton's Works; Ramsay's Philosophical Principles of natural and revealed Religion; Steven's Spanish Dictionary; Hutchinson's System of Moral Philosophy; and Jesuit's Practice of Perspective.

OCTAVO'S.

Bibles. A Complete History of England, from the Descent of Julius Caesar, to the Treaty of Aix la Chapelle, 1748. Containing the Transactions of One Thousand Eight Hundred and Three Years. By T. SMOLLETT, M. D. The Third Edition. London, Printed in the Year MDCCLVIII. Spirit of Laws; Burn's Justice (a Book of great Character) Brooks's Practice of Physic; Sharp's, Ledran's and Turner's Surgery; Swan's Sydenham; Every Man his own Lawyer; Ainsworth's Dictionary abridged: Ulloa's Voyage to South-America; Reading's Sermons; Bayly's Languages; Price on Morals; Extracts from Pausanaias; Jenny's Lectures in Anatomy; Dissenters System of Divinity; Whiston's Josephus; Burlamaqui on natural and politic Law; Sir William Temple's Work; Gravesend's and Roning's Philosophy; Warner's System of Morality and Divinity; Johnston's Dictionary. . . .

TWELVES.

The Naval History of Great Britain; with the most illustrious Admirals and Commanders, from the Reign of Queen Elizabeth. Interspersed with Accounts of the most important Discoveries made in the several Parts of the World; and including all the Great Events during the present War, to the Year One Thousand Seven Hundred and Fifty-eight. In four Volumes. Adorned with the Heads of the principal Admirals. London, Printed in the Year MDCCLVIII. Prior's Poems; Supplement to Pope's Works; Memoirs of a Protestant; The Herald; Spectator, Guardian, Tattler; Rambler; Modern Travels; Moliere's Works; Art of Preaching; Shakespear's Works. . . .

[From the *Boston News-Letter*, May 15-22, 1735]

To be Sold, at Mr. Smibert's, in Queen Street, on Monday, the 26th Instant, A Collection of valuable PRINTS, engrav'd by the best Hands, after the finest Pictures in Italy, France, Holland, and England, done by Raphael, Michael Angelo, Poussin, Rubens, and other the greatest Masters, containing a great Variety of Subjects, as History, etc, most of the Prints very rare, and not to be met with, except in private Collections: being what Mr. Smibert collected in the above-mentioned Countries, for his own private Use & Improvement: The Price of each single Print or Book to be mark'd upon 'em, and to be the same, which Mr. Smibert, who bought 'em at the best Hand, himself gave for them.

At the same Time, there will be Sold a Collection of Pictures in Oil Colours; the price of each Picture, to be mark'd upon it.

N. B. The Sale will last from Monday morning till the Saturday Evening following, and no longer: Those Prints, that shall remain then unsold, will be sent to England.

[From the *Pennsylvania Gazette*, May 24, 1759]

SAMUEL ALFORD. Jeweller and Goldsmith, late of Barbadoes, now in Lombard St., near the New Market, Philadelphia, Begs leave to inform the Publick, he intends to follow his Business in this Place. Self applause is needless, but a Trial in both those Branches, he doubts not will recommend him. His endeavors shall be to dispatch his Business with the utmost Expedition and the newest Fashions from England. Motto Rings made, engraved or enamelled, shall be completely done. The Friendship of all Gentlemen and Ladies and their Recommendation he would request while they find him honest. Their good will shall be esteemed as the highest Favor by their humble Servant Samuel Alford.

[From the *New York Gazette and the Weekly Mercury*, February 6, 1775]

SAMUEL PRINCE,
CABINET-MAKER,
At the Sign of the Chest of Drawers, in William-Street, near the North Church, in New York:

Makes and sells all sorts of cabinet work in the neatest manner, and on the lowest terms. Orders for the West Indies, and elsewhere, compleated, on the shortest notice. He has on hand, for sale,

A parcel of the most elegant furniture, made of mahogany, of the very best quality, such as chest of drawers, chest upon chest, cloath presses, desks, desks and book cases of different sorts, chairs of many different and new pattens, beuro tables, dining tables, card tables, breakfast tables, tea tables, And many other sorts of Cabinet work, very cheap.

[From the *New York Journal or the General Advertiser*, August 6, 1767]

CHARLES SHIPMAN, Ivory and Hardwood Turner, lately from England: Takes this Method to acquaint all ladies, gentlemen, &c. that having served a regular apprenticeship to a very considerable Turning Manufactory in Birmingham; he purposes carrying on that business here, in all the various undermentioned articles; Therefore all those who please to favour him with their employ, may depend on being served with the strictest assiduity, and on the most reasonable terms. Mahogany waiters and bottle stands, billiard balls, bell handles, cups and balls, dice boxes, pack thread boxes, pepper boxes, soap boxes, washball boxes, patch boxes, raisin boxes, glove sticks, drum sticks and walking stick heads, paste rollers, round rulers and sugar hammers, tobacco sieves, sand dishes, ivory totums, tooth-pick-cases and eggs, nutmeg graters, pounce boxes and ivory thimbles, ivory netting, and knotting needles; tobacco stoppers, and cases for smelling boxes, counting-house seal handles, and steel seals cut with cyphers, ivory counters engraved with alphabets and figures, (very popular for children) back gammons and chess men; Cruet frames repair'd and German flutes tip'd in the neatest manner, oval picture frames, and sundry other articles too tedious to mention.

VIII

Perspectives
and Predictions

To both native Americans and foreign visitors it was obvious that a bright future awaited Great Britain's New World colonies. Colonial America had enjoyed remarkable growth and prosperity; it had also begun to show signs of political maturity. Observers on both sides of the Atlantic began to wonder what shape that future would take.

During the third quarter of the eighteenth century many commentators articulated their predictions of the political, economic, and social fate of British America. Some observers—especially visiting Englishmen—read the past cautiously, seeing little in America's history to foreshadow drastic changes. Others—especially American colonists—viewed the previous century and a half as prologue to even more dramatic growth. A few prognosticators were remarkably accurate; most in the end proved wide of the mark.

But right or wrong, the habit of assessing America's past and predicting her future emerged as a characteristic element in the British colonies long before the rumblings of the Revolution had become audible. No one seemed immune to the temptation. Colonial leaders such as Franklin, temporary residents such as Hector St. John de Crevecoeur, and visitors such as the Reverend Andrew Burnaby all played the game of guessing America's destiny. (The mania for analysis and prediction continued long after the colonies achieved independence, reaching a climax in the nineteenth century with the observations of a peripatetic Frenchman, Alexis de Tocqueville.) But it was more than idle musing: the future of British America would be determined as much by what men foresaw (and thus desired and sought) as by acts of Parliament and ministerial decisions.

37.—HAPPINESS, NOT EMPIRE

In 1759 and 1760 the Reverend Andrew Burnaby, a Church of England clergyman, toured the American colonies. The account of his travels provides historians with a valuable record of eighteenth-century America; of equal interest are the "general reflections" with which he ended his narrative.—From Rufus Rockwell Wilson, ed., Burnaby's Travels Through North America (*New York, 1904), pp. 149-155.*

Having travelled over so large a tract of this vast continent, before I bid a final farewell to it, I must beg the reader's indulgence, while I stop for a moment, and as it were from the top of a high eminence, take one general retrospective look at the whole. An idea, strange as it is visionary, has entered into the minds of the generality of mankind, that empire is travelling westward; and every one is looking forward with eager and impatient expectation to that destined moment when America is to give law to the rest of the world. But if ever an idea was illusory and fallacious, I am fully persuaded, that this will be so.

America is formed for happiness, but not for empire: in a course of 1,200 miles I did not see a single object that solicited charity; but I saw insuperable causes of weakness, which will necessarily prevent its being a potent state.

Our colonies may be distinguished into the southern and northern, separated from each other by the Susquehanna and that imaginary line which divides Maryland from Pennsylvania.

The southern colonies have so many inherent causes of weakness, that they never can possess any real strength. The climate operates very powerfully upon them, and renders them indolent, inactive, and unenterprising; this is visible in every line of their character. I myself have been a spectator, and it is not an uncommon sight, of a man in the vigour of life, lying upon a couch, and a female slave standing over him, wafting off the flies, and fanning him, while he took his repose.

The southern colonies (Maryland, which is the smallest and most inconsiderable, alone excepted) will never be thickly seated: for as they are not confined within determinate limits, but extend to the westward indefinitely, men, sooner than apply to laborious occupations, occupations militating with their dispositions, and generally considered too as the inheritance and badge of slavery, will gradually retire westward, and settle upon fresh lands, which are said also to be more fertile; where, by the servitude of a negro or two, they may enjoy all the satisfaction of an easy and indolent independency: hence the lands upon the coast will of course remain thin of inhabitants.

The mode of cultivation by slavery, is another insurmountable cause of weakness. The number of negroes in the southern colonies is upon the whole nearly equal, if not superior, to that of the white men; and they propagate and increase even faster. Their condition is truly pitiable; their labour excessively hard, their diet poor and scanty, their treatment cruel and oppresive: they cannot therefore but be a subject of terror to those who so inhumanly tyrannize over them.

The Indians near the frontiers are a still further formidable cause of subjection. The southern Indians are numerous, and are governed by a sounder policy than formerly: experience has taught them wisdom. They never make war with the colonists without carrying terror and devastation along with them. They sometimes break up entire counties together. Such is the state of the southern colonies.

The northern colonies are of stronger stamina, but they have other difficulties and disadvantages to struggle with, not less arduous, or more easy to be surmounted, than what have been already mentioned. Their limits being defined, they will undoubtedly become exceedingly populous: for though men will readily retire back towards the frontiers of their own colony, yet they will not so easily be induced to settle beyond them, where different laws and polities prevail; and where, in short, they are a different people: but in proportion to want of teritory, if we consider the proposition in a general and abstract light, will be want of power. But the northern colonies have still more positive and real disadvantages to contend with. They are composed of people of different nations, different manners, different religions, and different languages. They have a mutual jealousy of each other, fomented by considerations of interest, power, and ascendancy. Religious zeal, too, like a smothered fire, is secretly burning in the hearts of the different sectaries that inhabit them, and were it not restrained by laws and superior authority, would soon burst out into a flame of universal persecution. Even the peaceable Quakers struggle hard for pre-eminence, and evince in a very striking manner that the passions of mankind are much stronger than any principles of religion.

The colonies, therefore, separately considered, are internally weak; but it may be supposed, that, by an union or coalition, they would become strong and formidable: but an union seems almost impossible: one founded in dominion or power is morally so: for, were not England to interfere, the colonies themselves so well understand the policy of preserving a balance, that, I think, they would not be idle spectators, were any one of them to endeavour to subjugate its next neighbour. Indeed, it appears to me a very doubtful point, even supposing all the colonies of America to be united under one head, whether it would be possible to keep in due order and government so wide and extended an empire, the difficulties of communication, of intercourse, of correspondence, and all other circumstances considered.

A voluntary association or coalition, at least a permanent one, is almost as difficult to be supposed: for fire and water are not more heterogeneous than the different colonies in North America. Nothing can exceed the jealousy and emulation which they possess in regard to each other. The inhabitants of Pennsylvania and New York have an inexhaustible source of animosity, in their jealousy for the trade of the Jerseys. Massachusetts Bay and Rhode Island, are not less interested in that of Connecticut. The West Indies are a common subject of emulation to them all. Even the limits and boundaries of each colony are a constant source of litigation. In short, such is the difference of character, of manners, of religion, of interest, of the different colonies, that I think, if I am not wholly ignorant of the human mind, were they left to themselves, there would soon be a civil war from one end of the continent to the other; while the Indians and negroes would, with better reason, impatiently watch the opportunity of exterminating them all together.

After all, however, supposing what I firmly believe will never take place, a permanent union or alliance of all the colonies, yet it could not be effectual, or productive of the event supposed; for such is the extent of coast settled by the American colonies that it can never be defended but by a maritime power: America must first be mistress of the sea before she can be independent, or mistress of herself. Suppose the colonies ever so populous; suppose them capable of maintaining 100,000 men constantly in arms, (a supposition in the highest degree extravagant), yet half a dozen frigates would with ease ravage and lay waste the whole country from end to end, without a possibility of their being able to prevent it; the country is so intersected by rivers, rivers of such magnitude as to render it impossible to build bridges over them, that all communication is in a manner cut off. An army under such circumstances could never act to any purpose or effect; its operations would be totally frustrated.

Further, a great part of the opulence and power of America depends upon her fisheries, and her commerce with the West Indies; she cannot subsist without them; but these would be entirely at the mercy of that power which might have the sovereignty of the seas. I conclude, therefore, that England, so long as she maintains her superiority in that respect, will also possess a superiority in America; but the moment she loses the empire of the one, she will be deprived of the sovereignty of the other: for were that empire to be held by France, Holland, or any other power, America, will, in all probability, be annexed to it. New establishments formed in the interior parts of America, will not come under this predicament; I should therefore think it the best policy to enlarge the present colonies, but not to establish fresh ones; for to suppose interior colonies to be of use to the mother country, by being a check upon those already settled, is to suppose what is contrary to experience, and the nature of things, viz. that men removed beyond the reach of power will be subordinate to it.

38.—"PAST, PRESENT, AND FUTURE"

Poor Richard's *was only the most famous of many colonial almanacs. In New England one of the most widely read came from the pen of Nathaniel Ames, of Dedham, Massachusetts. In addition to providing his readers with the usual meteorological and astronomical information, Ames entertained them with essays on a variety of subjects, mostly scientific. In the 1758 edition of his almanac, however, Ames turned to prophecy.—From Samuel Briggs, ed.,* The Essays, Humor, and Poems of Nathaniel Ames, Father and Son, . . . from their Almanacks, 1726-1775 *(Cleveland, 1891), pp. 284-286.*

A THOUGHT upon the past, present, *and* future State *of*
NORTH AMERICA.

America is a subject which daily becomes more and more interesting.—I shall therefore fill these Pages with a Word upon its Past,
Present and Future State.

I. First of its Past State: Time has cast a Shade upon this Scene.
—Since the Creation innumerable Accidents have happened here, the
bare mention of which would create Wonder and Surprize; but they
are all lost in Oblivion: The ignorant Natives for Want of Letters
have forgot their Stock; and know not from whence they came, or
how, or when they arrived here, or what has happened since:—Who
can tell what wonderful Changes have happen'd by the mighty Operations of Nature, such as Deluges, Vulcanoes, Earthquakes, &c.!—
Or whether great tracts of Land were not absorbed into those vast
Lakes or Inland Seas which occupy so much Space to the West of us.
—But to leave the Natural, and come to the Political State: We know
how the *French* have erected a Line of Forts from the *Ohio* to *Nova
Scotia,* including all the inestimable Country to the West of us, into
their exorbitant Claim.—This, with infinite Justice, the *English*
resented, & in this Cause our Blood has been spill'd: Which brings
to our Consideration,

II. Secondly, The Present State of NORTH AMERICA.—A
Writer upon this present Time says, "The Parts of *North America*
which may be claimed by *Great Britain* or *France* are of as much
Worth as either Kingdom.—That fertile Country to the West of the
Appalachian Mountains (a String of 8 or 900 Miles in Length,) between *Canada* and the *Mississippi,* is of larger Extent than all *France,
Germany* and *Poland;* and all well provided with Rivers, a very fine
wholesome Air, a rich Soil, capable of producing Food and Physick,
and all Things necessary for the Conveniency and Delight of Life: In
fine, the Garden of the World!"—Time was we might have been
possess'd of it: At this Time two mighty Kings contend for this
inestimable Prize:—Their respective Claims are to be measured by
the Length of their Swords.—The Poet says, The Gods and Opportunity ride Post; that you must take her by the Forelock being Bald
Behind.—Have we not too fondly depended upon our Numbers?—
Sir *Francis Bacon* says, "The Wolf careth not how many the Sheep
be:" But Numbers well spirited, with the Blessing of Heaven will do
Wonders, when by military Skill and Discipline, the Commanders can
actuate (as by one Soul) the most numerous bodies of arm'd People:

—Our Numbers will not avail till the Colonies are united; for whilst divided, the strength of the Inhabitants is broken like the petty Kingdoms in *Africa*.—If we do not join Heart and Hand in the common Cause against our exulting Foes, but fall to disputing among ourselves, it may really happen as the Governour of *Pennsylvania* told his Assembly, "We shall have no Priviledge to dispute about, nor Country to dispute in."—

III. Thirdly, of the Future State of NORTH AMERICA—Here we find a vast Stock of proper Materials for the Art and Ingenuity of Man to work upon:—Treasures of immense Worth; conceal'd from the poor ignorant aboriginal Natives! The Curious have observ'd, that the Progress of Humane Literature (like the Sun) is from the East to the West; thus has it travelled thro' *Asia* and *Europe,* and now is arrived at the Eastern Shore of *America.* As the Cœlestial Light of the Gospel was directed here by the Finger of GOD, it will doubtless, finally drive the long! long! Night of Heathenish Darkness from *America:*—So Arts and Sciences will change the Face of Nature in their Tour from Hence over the Appalachian Mountains to the Western Ocean; and as they march thro' the vast Desert, the Residence of Wild Beasts will be broken up, and their obscene Howl cease for ever;—Instead of which the Stones and Trees will dance together at the Music of *Orpheus,*—the Rocks will disclose their hidden Gems,—and the inestimable Treasures of Gold & Silver be broken up. Huge Mountains of Iron Ore are already discovered; and vast Stores are reserved for future Generations: This Metal more useful than Gold and Silver, will imploy Millions of Hands, not only to form the martial Sword, and peaceful Share, alternately; but an Infinity of Utensils improved in the Exercise of Art, and Handicraft amongst Men. Nature thro' all her Works has stamp'd Authority on this Law, namely, "That all fit Matter shall be improved to its best Purposes."—Shall not then those vast Quarries, that teem with mechanic Stone,—those for Structure be piled into great Cities,—and those for Sculpture into Statues to perpetuate the Honor of renowned Heroes; even those who shall NOW save their Country.—O! Ye unborn Inhabitants of America! Should this Page escape its destin'd Conflagration at the Year's End, and these Alphabetical Letters remain legible,—when your Eyes behold the Sun after he has rolled the Seasons round for two or three Centuries more, you will know that in Anno Domini 1758, we dream'd of your Times.

                                                    NATH. AMES.

39.—PROSPECTS OF POLITICAL
AND ECONOMIC INDEPENDENCE

*William Eddis served as Surveyor of Customs at Annapolis
and secretary to the governor of Maryland from 1769 to the
outbreak of the War for Independence. During that time he
wrote frequently to friends in England, describing the
scenes and events he witnessed. In two letters from Annapolis written in 1773, Eddis answered a correspondent's
request for information about American economic resources. In an earlier letter he had commented on the political future of the colonies. Extracts from these three
letters are presented here to give a coherent picture of
America's destiny as seen by a British functionary.—From
William Eddis,* Letters from America *(London, 1792), pp.
51-56, 139-144, 146, 149-150.*

Annapolis, April 2, 1770.

In a political point of view, independent of religious motives, it is
much to be lamented, that a plan [for the establishment of an Episcopal hierarchy in America] was not determined on, before the
colonies had arrived to their present degree of population and consequence: had an order of nobility been created, and dignitaries in the
church appointed at an early period, it would most assuredly have
greatly tended to cherish a steady adherence to monarchical principles; and have more strongly rivetted the attachment of the colonies
to the parent state. Inattention to principles of such importance, has
gradually given birth to sentiments totally repugnant to the genius
of our most excellent constitution. A republican spirit appears generally to predominate; and it will undoubtedly require the utmost
exertion of legislative wisdom, to establish on a permanent basis, the
future political and commercial connexion between Great Britain and
America.

There are many discerning and intelligent persons, who are de-
cidedly of opinion that the acquisition of Canada is highly prejudicial
to the interests of the mother country. The Americans are, by this

event, relieved from continual apprehensions; their frontiers are no longer exposed to the incursions of a restless enterprising neighbour; and they begin to encourage ideas of self-importance. . . .

Had Canada still continued annexed to the French empire, it is evident that the British provinces, from a well-grounded dread of such numerous and powerful opponents, must unavoidably, on a principle of self-preservation, if not of affection, have remained firmly and indissolubly attached to the parent state: a just apprehension of real calamities would have operated with efficacy against imaginary evils; and the natural and constitutional dependence of the colonies, on the protection and assistance of Great Britain, would have promoted a constant and mutual interchange of friendly and benevolent offices, which must have settled the union on a permanent foundation, and on terms reciprocally honourable and advantageous to both countries.

What will be the event of the present discontents, which, I am truly concerned to observe, are universally predominant, time alone can determine. There are amongst us, many restless spirits, who are evidently industrious in fomenting divisions, and exciting jealousies; and unless wise and constitutional measures are immediately adopted, there is too much reason to apprehend consequences of a serious and alarming nature.

Annapolis, Feb 20, 1773.

Your observations on the resources of America are well founded. I grant they are infinite, and I am persuaded that, in process of time, she will be enabled to avail herself of innumerable advantages; but those that assert she will effectually rival Great Britain in that invaluable staple of her commerce, the *woollen manufactory,* are, indeed, by far too sanguine in their expectations: coarse cloths for the wear of servants and negroes, the colonists may probably be enabled to manufacture, but insurmountable objections arise to the production of those of a superior quality.

To judge of this climate, by the parallel degrees of latitude in Europe, it is natural to conclude, that the middle provinces experience very little of the rigour of winter, and that, in fact, their greatest inconvenience must arise from intense heat, during the summer months. But, extraordinary as it may appear, this country, from local circumstances, is accustomed to every severity of the opposite seasons. I assure you, that I have been less sensible of the influence of the sun in the hottest seasons in the island of Jamaica, than in this part of British America; and I am credibly informed, that no material difference prevails from New York inclusive, to the southern extremity of Virginia. To the northward of New York the winters continue longer; the cold is equally intense; and the summer, for its short duration, hot in proportion. South of Virginia the climate gradually becomes similar to the torrid zone, consequently the wool degenerates, in a regular proportion, until the external covering of the sheep becomes at last a strong coarse hair resembling that of goats.

In Maryland, and in the adjacent provinces, the cold is more severe from January till the beginning of May, than in any part of the island of Great Britain; in consequence of which the American farmer is reduced to the necessity of housing his sheep during that rigid season. Summer may, literally, be said to be seated on the lap of winter, and the immediate transition from cold to heat is, evidently, extremely prejudicial to the growth and improvement of wool; so that in quality it is greatly inferior; nor is the quantity produced proportionable to what is yielded in the milder regions of the parent state.

Under these disadvantages it may reasonably be concluded, that the American settlements will ever be necessitated to look up to Britain for a very considerable supply of her invaluable staple. And even if these causes did not operate, many years must unavoidably elapse before the colonists can establish or conduct manufactures in such a manner, as to enable them to supply, even their own wants, on terms of greater advantage than by relying on external assistance.

This immense continent will require a considerable population before the inhabitants can, with any propriety, divert their attention from agriculture. To settle, and to cultivate lands must be their first great object; and the produce of those exertions they must barter in exchange for European manufactures. In vain is encouragement held forth, to induce ingenious artizans to emigrate from their original situations. On their arrival, either the allurements which tempted them deceive their expectations; or the natural wish to obtain a permanent establishment, supercedes every other consideration, and induces a great majority of these adventurers to purchase lands which, comparatively, bear no price, and the purchasers are reduced to rely on time and industry to recompence their assiduity.

Another circumstance, very important in its nature, likewise demands attention. The price of labour must be greatly lessened before the Americans can possibly manufacture to any advantage; and this inconvenience cannot be remedied, until, by an overplus of people, there are competitors in every art, and a sufficient number of opulent inhabitants to encourage and reward their ingenuity.

At present, it is evident, that almost every article of use or ornament, is to be obtained on much more reasonable terms from the mother country, than from artizans settled on this side the Atlantic. It is also as certain, that goods of every kind produced, or manufactured in England, are greatly superior to the produce or manufactures of this continent. In process of time, but a time far distant, the colonies may, undoubtedly, from their great resources, be enabled to rival Britain in many valuable articles of commerce. But in your grand staple, the growth and manufacture of wool, you will, in a general point of view, stand *single* and *pre-eminent.* . . .

Annapolis, Oct. 4, 1773.

. . . The legislature of this province, animated by sentiments which reflect the highest credit on their patriotism and wisdom, have . . . determined, by a recent law, to endow and found a college for the education of youth in every liberal and useful branch of science. An institution of this nature was most strongly recommended to their consideration by our worthy governor, at an early period after his arrival in this country; and to his laudable and persevering exertions, the public are materially indebted for the establishment of a seminary which, as it will be conducted under excellent regulations, will shortly preclude the necessity of crossing the Atlantic for the completion of a classical and polite education.

• • •

Institutions of this nature are inseparably connected with the interest and happiness of these provinces; but with respect to the parent state, they may possibly be attended with serious consequences. When the real, or supposed necessity ceases of sending the youth of this continent to distant seminaries for the completion of their education, the attachment of the colonies to Great Britain will gradually weaken, and a less frequent intercourse will tend to encourage those sentiments of self-importance which have already taken too deep root, and which, I fear, the utmost exertions of political wisdom will never be able wholly to eradicate. As an Englishman I therefore cannot but view, with a partial regret, every adopted plan that may possibly, in the event, lessen or alienate the affection of the colonists. And though I am sensible the good of the whole ought to supercede every private consideration, yet I cannot anticipate the future importance and prosperity of America, without a most fervent prayer, that every advantage she may derive from her exertions, may ultimately depend on a permanent and constitutional connexion with the mother country.

40.—A NEW SOCIETY

One of the most articulate philosophers of America's destiny, Hector St. John de Crevecoeur, was interested not only in institutions and individuals but in society as a whole. Shortly before the outbreak of the Revolutionary War, Crevecoeur recorded his conviction that America had already produced a new type of man and a new form of society—both, he contended, superior to their European counterparts. His famous essay, "What is an American," explained how Europeans became Americans; it also implied the emergence of an American nationalism and predicted that the new American society would someday provide inspiration and leadership for the rest of mankind.— From Hector St. John de Crevecoeur, Letters from an American Farmer (New York, 1908), pp. 76-80, 52-55.

An European, when he first arrives, seems limited in his intentions, as well as in his views; but he very suddenly alters his scale; two hundred miles formerly appeared a very great distance, it is now but a trifle; he no sooner breathes our air than he forms schemes, and embarks in designs he never would have thought of in his own country. There the plenitude of society confines many useful ideas, and often extinguishes the most laudable schemes which here ripen into maturity. Thus Europeans become Americans.

But how is this accomplished in that croud of low, indigent people, who flock here every year from all parts of Europe? I will tell you; they no sooner arrive than they immediately feel the good effects of that plenty of provisions we possess: they fare on our best food, and are kindly entertained; their talents, character, and peculiar industry are immediately inquired into; they find countrymen every where disseminated, let them come from whatever part of Europe. Let me select one as an epitome of the rest; he is hired, he goes to work, and works moderately; instead of being employed by a haughty person, he finds himself with his equal, placed at the substantial table of the farmer, or else at an inferior one as good; his wages are high, his bed is not like that bed of sorrow on which he used to lie: if he behaves with propriety, and is faithful, he is caressed, and becomes as it were a member of the family. He begins to feel the effects of a sort of resurrection; hitherto he had not lived, but simply vegetated; he now feels himself a man, because he is treated as such; the laws of his own country had overlooked him in his insignificancy; the laws of this cover him with their mantle. Judge what an alteration there must arise in the mind and thoughts of this man; he begins to forget his former servitude and dependence, his heart involuntarily swells and glows; this first swell inspires him with those new thoughts which constitute an American. What love can he entertain for a country where his existence was a burthen to him; if he is a generous good man, the love of this new adoptive parent will sink deep into his heart. He looks around, and sees many a prosperous person, who but a few years before was as poor as himself. This encourages him much, he begins to form some little scheme, the first, alas, he ever formed in his life. If he is wise he thus spends two or three years, in which time he acquires knowledge, the use of tools, the modes of working the lands, felling trees, &c. This prepares the foundation of a good name, the most useful acquisition he can make. He is encouraged, he has gained friends; he is advised and directed, he feels bold, he purchases some land; he gives all the money he has brought over, as well as what he has earned, and trusts to the God of harvests for the discharge of the rest. His good name procures him credit. He is now possessed of the deed, conveying to him and his posterity the fee simple and absolute property of two hundred acres of land, situated on such a river. What an epocha in this man's life! He is become a freeholder, from perhaps a German boor—he is now an American, a Pennsylvanian, an English subject. He is naturalized, his name is enrolled with those of the other citizens of the province. Instead of being a vagrant, he has a place of residence; he is called the inhabitant of such a county, or of such a district, and for the first time in his life counts for something; for hitherto he has been a cypher. I only repeat what I have heard many say, and no wonder their hearts should glow, and be agitated with a multitude of feelings, not easy to describe. From nothing to start into being; from a servant to the rank of a master; from being the slave of some despotic prince, to become a free man, invested with lands, to which every municipal blessing is annexed! What a change indeed! It is in consequence of that change that he becomes an American. This great metamorphosis has a double effect, it extinguishes all his European prejudices, he forgets that mechanism of subordination, that servility of disposition which poverty had taught him; and sometimes he is apt to forget too much, often passing from one extreme to the other. If he is a good man, he forms schemes of future prosperity, he proposes to educate his children better than he has been educated himself; he thinks of future modes of conduct, feels an ardor to labour he never felt before. Pride steps in and leads him to every thing that the laws do not forbid: he respects them; with a heart-felt gratitude he looks toward the east, toward that insular government from whose wisdom all his new felicity is derived, and under whose wings and protection he now lives. These reflections constitute him the good man and the good subject. Ye poor Europeans, ye, who sweat, and work for the great—ye, who are obliged to give so many sheaves to the church, so many to your lords, so many to your government, and have hardly any left for yourselves—ye, who are held in less estimation than favourite hunters or useless lap-dogs—ye, who only breathe the air of nature, because it cannot be withheld from you; it is here that ye can conceive the possibility of those feelings I have been describing; it is here the laws of naturalization invite every one to partake of our great labours and felicity, to till unrented, untaxed lands! . . .

•   •   •

In this great American asylum, the poor of Europe have by some means met together, and in consequence of various causes; to what purpose should they ask one another what countrymen they are? Alas, two thirds of them had no country. Can a wretch who wanders about, who works and starves, whose life is a continual scene of sore affliction or pinching penury; can that man call England or any other kingdom his country? A country that had no bread for him, whose fields procured him no harvest, who met with nothing but the frowns of the rich, the severity of the laws, with jails and punishments; who owned not a single foot of the extensive surface of this planet? No! urged by a variety of motives, here they came. Every thing has tended to regenerate them; new laws, a new mode of living, a new social system; here they are become men: in Europe they were as so many useless plants, wanting vegitative mould, and refreshing showers; they withered, and were mowed down by want, hunger, and war; but now by the power of transplantation, like all other plants they have taken root and flourished! Formerly they were not numbered in any civil lists of their country, except in those of the poor; here they rank as citizens. By what invisible power has this surprising metamorphosis been performed? By that of the laws and that of their industry. The laws, the indulgent laws, protect them as they arrive, stamping on them the symbol of adoption; they receive ample rewards for their labours; these accumulated rewards procure them lands; those lands confer on them the title of freemen, and to that title every benefit is affixed which men can possibly require. This is the great operation daily performed by our laws. From whence proceed these laws? From our government. Whence the government? It is derived from the original genius and strong desire of the people ratified and confirmed by the crown. This is the great chain which links us all, this is the picture which every province exhibits. . . .

What attachment can a poor European emigrant have for a country where he had nothing? The knowledge of the language, the love of a few kindred as poor as himself, were the only cords that tied him: his country is now that which gives him land, bread, protection, and consequence: *Ubi panis ibi patria,* is the motto of all emigrants. What then is the American, this new man? He is either an European, or the descendant of an European, hence that strange mixture of blood, which you will find in no other country. I could point out to you a family whose grandfather was an Englishman, whose wife was Dutch, whose son married a French woman, and whose present four sons have now four wives of different nations. *He* is an American, who leaving behind him all his ancient prejudices and manners, receives new ones from the new mode of life he has embraced, the new government he obeys, and the new rank he holds. He becomes an American by being received in the broad lap of our great *Alma Mater.* Here individuals of all nations are melted into a new race of men, whose labours and posterity will one day cause great changes in the world. Americans are the western pilgrims, who are carrying along with them that great mass of arts, sciences, vigour, and industry which began long since in the east; they will finish the great circle. . . .